THE
BACKROAD
CHRONICLES

ADVENTURE & HISTORY
IN BRITISH COLUMBIA

VOLUME ONE

By
Riel Marquardt

Cover, map and page design by Greg Sue and Riel Marquardt.

Photo Credits:
All photographs by Riel Marquardt except as follows:
Vancouver Public Library: pp 100, 116, 170.
Greg Sue: rear cover.

Note for Librarians: A cataloguing record for this book is available from Library and Archives Canada at www.collectionscanada.ca/amicus/index-e.html
ISBN 1-4120-5903-8

Printed in Victoria, BC, Canada. Printed on paper with minimum 30% recycled fibre.
Trafford's print shop runs on "green energy" from solar, wind and other environmentally-friendly power sources.

TRAFFORD
PUBLISHING™
Offices in Canada, USA, Ireland and UK

Book sales for North America and international:
Trafford Publishing, 6E–2333 Government St.,
Victoria, BC V8T 4P4 CANADA
phone 250 383 6864 (toll-free 1 888 232 4444)
fax 250 383 6804; email to orders@trafford.com
Book sales in Europe:
Trafford Publishing (UK) Limited, 9 Park End Street, 2nd Floor
Oxford, UK OX1 1HH UNITED KINGDOM
phone +44 (0)1865 722 113 (local rate 0845 230 9601)
facsimile +44 (0)1865 722 868; info.uk@trafford.com
Order online at:
trafford.com/05-0804

10 9 8 7 6 5 4 3

Partial net proceeds from the sale of this book will be donated to Ducks Unlimited Canada to aid in wetland conservation for North American waterfowl.

Dedicated To

Digby, watching us from high up on the mountain.

Acknowledgements

Countless thanks to Kari and Lucy, Sprocket, Greg, Jim, Michael, Darcy and Dawn.

Disclaimer

On backroads your safety is your responsibility... period. Preparation and experience reduce risk but cannot eliminate it. If you doubt your ability to drive infrequently maintained or non-maintained roads, handle emergency vehicle repairs, deal with wild animal encounters or respond to sudden medical emergencies, seek the company of someone that does or obtain training before you venture out.

The author and publisher disclaim liability for any injury and/or loss by anyone using information in this book.

What This Book Is, What It Is Not

This book is a collection of our more memorable trail adventures discovered in our less than modern, but trusty, four-wheel drive along the remote backroads and locations of southern British Columbia.

It is not a detailed, step by step guidebook to backroad trails. Since roads and reference points in BC's backroad country can vary significantly from one month to the next, much less from year to year, they often prove unreliable for future route finding by the reader. I have refrained from specifically rating the four-wheel drive sections of our travels. In my experience, a challenging piece of trail that causes one driver to panic and run screaming from his vehicle might not even cause another to think twice. Type of vehicle, seat time behind the wheel, weather conditions, pre-trip planning and plain luck make considerable differences to every backroad experience. However, I do note the trips in this book that are known as serious four-wheel drive trails, likely requiring vehicle modifications and/or a winch. These should only be attempted by experienced backroad drivers who are aware of their vehicle's limitations, and not alone.

It is our hope that this book will entertain those readers that may never have a chance to explore the backroad country of BC. For those readers able to embark upon backroad adventures of their own, whether in BC or elsewhere, may this book inspire and awaken the adventurer within you. We hope you enjoy.

Riel, Karen & Keera

iv

Contents

Trip Chapters

Introduction

How did we get so lucky? That is the question that Karen and I repeatedly ask ourselves when we return from a backroad adventure in BC. I sense our German Shepherd, Keera, does too! As we explore the backroads and trails of British Columbia we are fascinated by the province's past. By retracing the steps of BC's pioneers, it is my intention to make history come alive for you in this book. I want to introduce you to the people who lived here before us: dedicated individuals who laid the framework for our present travel routes, town sites and resulting quality of life.

The natural beauty of this province plays no small part in our addiction to backroad travel. To be an outdoor enthusiast and Nature lover and to live in what is the most diverse wilderness Eden of Canada is truly a gift to be thankful for. It is the kind of beauty that is difficult to put into words and impossible to capture on film, though I have tried.

Consider this: within a day's drive the average British Columbian can choose backroads that link the ocean, coastal rain forests, snow-covered mountain peaks, arid deserts, pristine alpine waters, rolling upland plateaus and countless flora and fauna species. The list is endless. Remember to practice 'no trace camping' and leave your discoveries as you found them for all future visitors.

Safety First

As with most outdoor activities, backroad travel is a pursuit where self-education, planning and knowledge are key. Please note the following points.

1) Ensure your vehicle is in peak condition. Be proactive in your vehicle maintenance. For example, if your battery is five years old, replace it now. Don't wait for it to potentially fail on the trail.

2) Travel with a companion vehicle. If one vehicle breaks down, or one driver is injured, the second vehicle can drive out for help.

3) Carry vehicle essentials, such as an inflated spare tire, mag lock keys, spare fuel, wrenches, etc.

4) Join a four-wheel drive club. This will allow for companionship while travelling with other experienced drivers and foster your own knowledge level.

5) Educate yourself. Study maps of the areas you want to explore. The internet is a vast source of information. One of the busiest four-wheel drive web pages is BC4X4.com. Before you head out on a new trail ask on the message board if anyone has any knowledge of the conditions of the trail or the area.

6) The most common vehicles you are likely to encounter on Forestry backroads are loaded logging trucks. Pay attention to, and obey, all warning signs. Pull off the road when heavy equipment approaches. If you have a VHF radio you can monitor logging traffic by entering the logging frequency posted on Forestry road signs, usually located at the start of logging roads.

7) Leave your itinerary, especially if you are travelling solo. Even in a group, it is wise to have a responsible person at home to be aware if you do not return on time.

Let me reiterate that a successful and safe four-wheel backroad trip starts with knowledge and planning *before* you leave for the trailhead.

Respect and Responsibility

Though BC's wilderness may appear endless, it is not. The human species, with its ever-burgeoning population, truly does affect every corner of the globe, whether intentionally or unintentionally. Therefore, we need to strive to keep our individual impact to a minimum.

In the city neighbourhood in which you live you need to act responsibly, respect your fellow citizens and obey society's laws. In Nature's neighbourhood it is no different: excessive noise and air pollution, maliciously travelling off the beaten path thereby destroying alpine meadows and other vegetation, littering and feeding wild animals, are against Nature's laws and fortunately, in many cases, against human laws. While exploring any backroad trail please treat Nature's house and its wildlife inhabitants with the utmost respect. Be aware that you are entering a vast and ancient architecture that has taken thousands of years to perfect.

Be responsible for minimising your mark upon it. Human health, yours and mine, is far more dependent on a healthy, natural environment than most of us take the time to realise.

What Is A Backroad?

To me a backroad has a promise attached to it... a promise of excitement and adventure. It beckons to me and begs me to question: 'Why is it here? Where does it go? What will I see?'

In more literal terms, a backroad in my book is any unpaved road surface that is not under regular repair and maintenance. A backroad, as is any travel route, is subject to constant change from one season to the next or one day to the next. But, unlike a major paved highway, no immediate maintenance crews are assigned to ensure safe and continuous travel for the motoring public.

These constant road changes, which are part of the adventure of exploring backroads, demand certain responsibilities and precautions on behalf of the backroad explorer to ensure his or her safety. Some, but not all, of these safety precautions and responsibilities are detailed in the 'Safety First' and 'Respect and Responsibility' sections of this book.

Do I Really Need A Four-Wheel Drive?

Depending on the time of year and amount of road maintenance provided, many roads in this collection may not require four-wheel drive at all. I remember discussing with several college students at a wilderness lodge in the Chilcotin, our journey over a muddy 6000-foot mountain pass earlier that day in our four-wheel drive. One girl indicated they too had passed it that day... in their Honda Civic!

Though this two-wheel drive vehicle may not have been the safest means of transportation for the pass, and the girls did admit to some periods of elevated anxiety, it did deliver its occupants to the other side.

The primary benefits of most, but not all, four-wheel drive vehicles are higher road clearance, added traction control and undercarriage skid plates. These are prime considerations to help reduce damage potential to the vehicle and add peace of mind for drivers when travelling roads or trails that are washed out, cross-ditched, and minimally maintained.

Maps

Please note that all my maps in this book are not to scale and do not indicate every side road. These maps should be used for general reference purposes only.

In my experience there is no definitive source for 100% accurate backroad trails and byways. The number of trails and constant changes taking place are simply too numerous to monitor. However, some map sources are better than others.

I have made use of topographical maps issued by the Department of Energy, Mines and Resources which, in the 1:50,000 scale, provide reasonable resolution and provide latitude and longitude information for reference with a GPS unit. They are sold at government agencies, bookstores and now online. Note that some of these maps may date back to the 1970s and could, therefore, be hopelessly out of date. You can verify dates for specific maps on the internet.

Another excellent map source is the Mussio Venture Backroad Mapbook Series available at most bookstores and online. If your pocketbook allows for it, there are now many software maps that can be purchased and downloaded directly into your GPS unit.

Your comments and trip suggestions are welcome. Please visit our website: www.bcbackroads.ca.

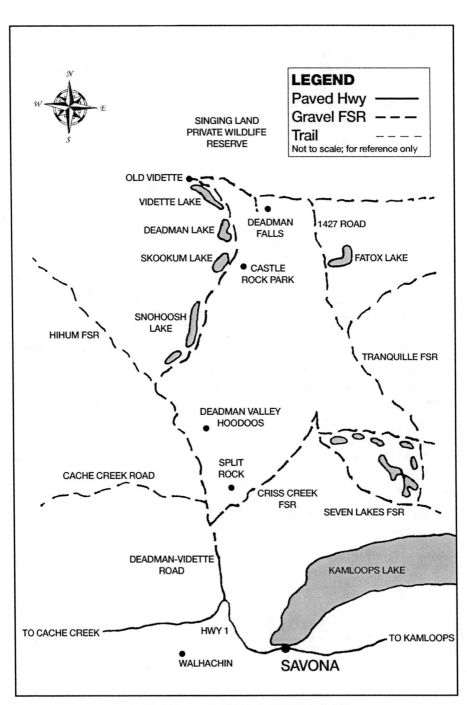

DEADMAN - CRISS CREEK LOOP

Deadman Bound

...required a certain degree of fitness and agility to climb; being part mountain goat would be beneficial.

In the Beginning...

For over four decades I had driven past the mysterious Deadman Valley Road turn-off and never ventured down it. As a child, in the back seat of my parents' car, I would peer into the entrance of the valley as we drove by it on our annual summer vacation trip to the 'Sunny Okanagan' from 'Up North'. The rugged Deadman scenery stirred up boyhood images of the Wild West: warriors riding bareback on mustangs, and dust covered cowboys herding their longhorns into the searing heat of a desert day. My parents, preoccupied with arriving at a predetermined place by a predetermined time, were oblivious to the treasures that a young boy knew lay down a valley with such an intriguing name. Later, as an adult with liberty to stop where and when I desired, I found myself only staring curiously into the valley turn-off during my infrequent drive-bys. Now I was the one always en-route to a predetermined destination for a predetermined time, always having more important matters at hand, always too busy to stop and explore the Deadman Valley secrets.

The turn-off for Deadman Valley is between Kamloops and Cache Creek on Highway 1, just west of Savona. My research indicated that the Deadman Creek and Deadman Valley names date back to the Gold Rush days of the 1860s. Prior to this time the area's rather gloomy namesakes were recorded as the Rivière des Défunts (River of the Dead) as well as Knife River.

Riel Marquardt

History states that a French-Canadian clerk named Charette, of the nearby North West Fur Company post, Fort Kamloops, was murdered in the early 1800s by his travel companion. Apparently the two became embroiled in an argument over where to rest for the night and the companion's knife settled the dispute forcefully and permanently.

Now that I knew the historical background of Deadman Valley, my desire to explore its reaches was rekindled. I promised myself to move from spectator to participant. One day it happened. The stars aligned and a date was set for a backroad trip into Deadman Valley. Karen and I decided on a circle tour; we would start at the southern end of Deadman Road, signposted the Deadman-Vidette Road, then head north. Once at valley's end we would climb onto the Cariboo Plateau and find a quiet lake to camp for the evening. The plan was to head in a southern direction the next morning, exploring old trails and following the Criss Creek FSR (Forest Service Road) until we rejoined the Deadman Valley Road.

The wildlife we viewed on this trip proved to be varied and continuous: an immature Bald Eagle fishing on the creek, a nesting Osprey pair feeding its young family, and a brief glimpse of a rare Great Gray Owl. Countless duck species bobbed along undisturbed lakeshores (sure to quicken any bird watcher's pulse), including Buffleheads, Goldeneyes, Wood Ducks and Mergansers. Larger mammals, such as bear and moose, graced our short two day visit to this country.

The natural beauty of the Deadman Valley and its surrounding areas offers sanctuary to all residents. Some of our stops included a hidden water fall, meadows carpeted in wildflowers, numerous secluded fishing lakes, ancient geological formations including hoodoos and a giant natural sand castle.

We followed the tracks of the early fur traders, gold seekers and modern logging companies. The Deadman backroads facilitated our passage through this wonderful land. This valley receives minimal annual precipitation so the best time to travel in my opinion, is in the spring. During this season the landscape explodes with contrasts; the greening plant life and the varied shades of reds, blues and browns that dominate the geology of the surrounding rock outcrops and cliffs all compete for top colour credits along Deadman Road.

The valley trends north, like a long wedge, increasing in elevation until it merges with the Bonaparte Plateau in the Cariboo. At the southern end ranches are randomly spaced, their fertile lands cover the valley up to the rim-rock on both sides of the creek. Further up the valley the farm lands are displaced, the lakes and forests fill the narrowing valley bottom. The area's scenery is perhaps the loveliest within the entire Thompson Valley system – and not a motel or fast food outlet to be found.

Joining us on this trip was Jud Barnes. Jud is a man well known for his life-long passion of exploring the backroads of BC. His calm, comprehending gaze immediately reveals his quiet confidence and peaceful nature. Tall and lean, with thick black hair and a full beard, his appearance suggests that of a rugged prospector who has just stepped out of an 1860s Gold Rush photo. His great love of the outdoors has helped him discover untold trails in BC during the last thirty years. Even though he lives in the metropolis of Vancouver, Jud is most at home outside the city, preferably exploring a remote area of BC in his veteran four-wheel drive. His many years of off-road experience, eagerness to attempt the toughest of trails, uncanny ability to recall the tiniest details of long forgotten routes, self-sufficiency skills and above all willingness to help and share with others, have earned Jud the much-deserved respect of the four-wheel drive community in BC. This man's trip logs could fill countless volumes. Karen and I were delighted and knew Jud to be a welcome companion on any backroad trip.

Finally, I was Deadman bound.

On the Trail...

It was early Saturday morning in the last week of May. The dew hung heavy upon the roadside grasses. The sun emerged from behind the eastern mountains as we rounded the last bend on Highway 1 before the Deadman Valley Road turn-off. With utter delight I signalled to take the Deadman exit. I felt great. The truck was running perfectly and the weather forecast was in our favour. After we located Jud over the VHF radio, we met several kilometres up Deadman Valley Road, where the pavement ended and the gravel started. All around us armies of sagebrush and junipers stood guard as if to report our intrusion into this story book setting. A rare recent rainfall had allowed the plants to fill the air with their scent. On the western slopes, the remains of wooden flumes that once carried the

Looking south down Deadman Valley

life-giving waters of Deadman Creek from the various upland lakes to the orchards of the ghost town of Walhachin (Native for 'Land of Plenty') were still visible. This 50-acre town site, located above the Thompson River several kilometres downstream from the valley, was the brainchild of an American engineer and a British nobleman. Started in 1907, it saw development of 3000 acres of arid sagebrush land into fruit producing orchards. However with the outbreak of WWI in 1914, all able-bodied men left for the front. Without the proper labour resources to operate and maintain the flumes and ditches that stretched over 120 miles, the orchards and the town were doomed. After a few short years and millions of dollars invested, Walhachin soon joined ranks with other ghost towns in BC.

We then passed through the Skeetchestn Band village. The many beautiful steeds that were playing, galloping and grazing adjacent to the road attested to the fact that this was horse-lover country. At the 12km mark we passed the Criss Creek FSR. We would emerge here a day later.

Several kilometres later, we admired the red lava cliffs where the valley narrows to a canyon. Millions of years old, the red and purple formations are the first of several geological wonders in this valley. To the left, a trail emerged. Jud mentioned he had travelled it numerous times in past decades, indicating it to be a pleasant backroad excursion as it passed several lakes before descending into Cache Creek.

At the next ranch we were granted the opportunity to observe an immature Bald Eagle, its youth evident by its lack of white head and tail feathers. It sat high in a dead tree by the creek, facing away from us. The eagle rhythmically moved its head from side to side, its brown and black feathers glistening in the sunshine. Even at our distance without binoculars we could make out the deep yellow beak occasionally snapping at airborne pests. At first we assumed it had its intentions on some nearby ranch chickens. We soon realised it was patiently waiting for breakfast to swim down Deadman Creek, its eyes ever-watchful for that promising silver glint, its body eager for the perfect moment to pluck a delicious meal out of the flow. Occasionally the raptor would switch positions in the old tree.

When it faced us, we were able to relish the true magnificence of this bird. We had binoculars in hand now and examined it in every detail while it patiently waited. It appeared to be a poor fishing day for the eagle, or perhaps it was just particular about its meal size. Eventually our timetable drove us on, the eagle's schedule more timeless than our own.

Several kilometres further, after a small hill and a bend in the road there was a red sign at a pullout that marked the next geological marvel of this valley, the Deadman Hoodoos. With a

Climbing to the Hoodoos... it helps to be part mountain goat

little searching they were visible with binoculars on the eastern slopes. Access to these ancient and quiet sentries was across private land. We acquired a contact number and phoned the rancher before we arrived. He allowed us to park on his property and access his bridge across Deadman Creek. The two hour trek required a certain degree of fitness and agility to climb; being part mountain goat would be beneficial, as the trail was steep and unmarked.

However when one perseveres, these ancient and seemingly

Karen, Jud and Keera in front of the Deadman Hoodoos

gravity-defying structures of Nature are a wonder to behold. Each clay and gravel column is forty to fifty feet high with a large slab of rock precariously balanced on top. We cautiously picked our way to the base of the statues, making sure not to dislodge any key rocks that might cause their undoing, not to mention bury us under tons of rock. As we peered straight up at the columns it seemed impossible that Nature could engineer such a structure without the aid of man-made re-bar and complex calculus equations.

Hoodoos are formed by erosion, the gradual wearing down

of land by a combination of water, wind and ice over millions of years. Since the top, or 'cap', of a hoodoo is composed of a different and slower eroding material than the tower portion of the hoodoo, it actually protects the entire structure and prevents it from collapsing. However, as erosion is a never-ending process the Deadman Hoodoos will one day crumble and disappear, perhaps tomorrow or in another thousand years.

After a break and plenty of pictures we picked our way back down the hillside.

Abandoned log house

Back at our vehicles we thanked the rancher and continued northward up Deadman Road. At the 20km marker Old Hihium Lake Road veered to the left, which my map book indicated to be four-wheel access only. Initially, I had wanted to lock the hubs and explore this road. Jud, however, indicated that since the pipeline had been buried here the road had been improved

and 'was no longer worthy of a true four-wheel drive experience'. We therefore carried on with our original plan up the
valley.

Castle Rock

The valley gradually narrowed with hay fields giving way
to forest and lakes. As the valley narrowed so did the road. It
now had many blind spots and our speed dropped accordingly.
We passed numerous cabins and homesteads, some inhabited,
others long abandoned.

The Forest Recreation Site at Snohoosh Lake was deserted,
despite the fine weather and weekend day. Unlike the other
lakes in the area this site had fine beach access for shore fishing.

East of Skookum Lake we explored the next geological odd-
ity along this intriguing valley. Named 'Castle Rock' by the
locals, a large tan coloured cliff face has been sculpted by Nature's elements into a Disney-style castle. One expected to see

a fair maiden beckoning her prince to come rescue her from atop one of the large limestone turrets. This rock formation was deemed significant enough for the government to designate it a tiny provincial park, as evidenced by a weatherworn and barely visible signpost leaning sideways, surrounded by brush. At noon we had lunch in the shade of a tree. After a lengthy siesta we located a steep access trail to the top of the castle, giving us a bird's eye view of the valley. Though we did not find any maidens in distress, bluebells were growing everywhere at the summit.

Crossing mud holes to Deadman Falls

Just north of Castle Rock was Deadman Lake and the Deadman Forest Recreation Site, also deserted. We passed Vidette Lake, the final lake in the valley. Its shores teemed with a wide variety of ducks and other waterfowl, a birdwatcher's paradise. Several private cabins overlooked the southern end of the lake while the Vidette Gold Mine Resort watched over the northern end. This resort location was inhabited as early as the 1840s by the fur trading staff of the Hudson's Bay Company. Apparently the resort reconstructed a cabin from the original HBC outpost. The Vidette Gold Mine originally opened with much promise in the 1930s. It was soon shut down when the lofty expectations did not materialise. We asked at the resort for access to the mine but were informed that access was limited to paying guests only.

Back on the gravel road we continued north, the switchbacks we encountered marked the end of the Deadman Valley and Thompson country. Ahead of us now lay the Bonaparte Plateau, part of the larger Cariboo Plateau. The scenery mellowed to a mixture of rolling meadows blotted with aspen and cottonwood tree stands and the occasional pine. The sharp contrasts returned suddenly. We were treated to a colour explosion, as if Van Gough's paintbrush itself had lost control. Millions of blue wild flowers, with infrequent yellow and red plant intruders, covered the meadows around us. Every bend, every rise offered our eyes more: Indian paintbrushes, asters, lupines and geraniums. These beautiful meadows, appropriately named the 'Singing Lands', are part of a private wild life reserve and were therefore fenced. Respectful of the 'No Trespassing' signs, we took our pictures from the road's edge.

The Deadman Falls entrance was not marked but the roar of the falls announced the turn-off. Jud led us through a maze of large mud holes, to what once was a small Forest Recreation Site.

The last distance had to be covered on foot. Signs along the trail warned of the unprotected canyon rim and to secure children and pets. A slip would prove fatal. The thundering spring runoff hurtles over the 150-foot plus vertical cliff at the apex of a magnificent canyon. Hard to believe that by August the water flow is just a trickle, barely enough to keep the rocks wet. Here at the lip of the gorge were more post-card photo images. I became aware of the dampness and immediacy of the waterfall spray, and instinctively stepped back a few feet. Anyone suffering from vertigo is best to limit their approach. We carefully snapped a photo album worth of pictures and continued on in our trucks.

Deadman Falls

Several more ranch buildings on a buffalo farm appeared as we continued to head east, Jud leading by several minutes. A black bear limbered across the way, perhaps fifteen feet away. As is often the case for me, by the time I had the camera set it had swiftly returned to its safe zone, across a gully and halfway up a steep embankment. The bruin rose on its hind legs, and sniffed the air. I contemplated getting out of the truck for a closer shot, but only for a moment. The sight of an equally shiny black cub ahead of its mother made me reconsider. We lost sight of the sow and cub as they clambered up the slope into the underbrush, their glistening coats evidence of the area's abundant food stores or as Karen called it the 'Bonaparte Buffet'. Not a minute later we passed a small lake and disturbed a magnificent cow moose and her offspring. They hesitated briefly, then bolted for forest cover. Nature's instinct led them to safety within the dark brush. Karen thanked Jud on the radio for leaving us all this wildlife to observe. He radioed back that all he saw was the occasional cow.

At a four-way intersection we turned right onto newer logging roads which Jud had not travelled before. They were constructed over the older, less defined trails that Jud was familiar with. We followed the wide new road for several kilometres. As it was approaching dinnertime, we decided to camp at the next lake. Jud indicated that he had camped there many years previously. We followed him down a small cart track. The map indicated Fatox Lake. It was deserted, undeveloped and hidden from view, the perfect place to spend the night.

As if on cue, rain started to fall as we exited our trucks to choose our camp spot. We agreed on a site not far from the water's edge that provided maximum forest canopy coverage for added rain protection and tree trunks to anchor our tarps. We circled our wagons and unloaded the overnight gear. While clearing some underbrush for our tent site I sensed movement above me. As I turned my head up sideways, my torso still hunched over, I caught glimpse of a Great Gray, the most elusive of all the owl species. As if suspended by a magical string from the sky, the large bird hovered, frozen in mid-air immediately above me, its enormous round face calm and inquisitive. Bright yellow eyes looked straight down at me for the briefest of moments. Then, without a whisper, it continued to effortlessly sail past me into a grove of trees and vanished. I stood

Camping in the rain at Fatox Lake

up, straight as an arrow. I stared at length at the very spot in which the stealthy acrobat had disappeared. Had I just imagined that? I looked over to my travel companions for support: Karen had her back to me preparing dinner; Jud was deep inside his truck searching for something. Even our dog Keera, with her radar-like hearing, faced the opposite direction. She guarded the entrance way, and obviously had not heard a sound.

I had no witnesses. I stared again at the owl's vanishing point, still left speechless by its aerial abilities. I never heard nor saw another sign of this rare nocturnal bird during our stay at Fatox Lake.

Some North American Native cultures worshipped the owl as an idol, believing it to have great healing powers, while others believed it to have ties to darkness, representing a reincarnation of the devil. I decided to align myself with the former belief.

Fortunately the rain fell only as cloudbursts that night. We enjoyed a cozy campsite, relaxing after dinner around the crackling campfire while sitting under the protective tarps and tree canopy. Deep into the night our laughter echoed through the damp woods, only heard by unseen creatures. Once in our sleeping bags, the night was black, pitch black, and accompanied by utter and complete silence. Ah, heaven. I slept deeper that night than I had in months.

As we broke camp the next morning, the rains had stopped though the skies were still grey and threatening. Jud led us down the logging Main for several more kilometres and then turned right. He was looking for an old trail that led to a small lake and cabin. Both sides of the trail were recently logged and left behind a totally bare landscape. Only partially burned slash piles hinted at the trees that had been harvested here lately. We took several side roads that did not trigger Jud's legendary memory. We returned to the Main and explored further turnoffs. Then Jud radioed to tell us he found the trail. We followed him and disappeared into the undergrowth, leaving the wide-open scars of the freshly logged hills behind us. On both sides of us, three- and four-foot round log stumps were left from logging the old growth forest many years ago. Today's loggers would be lucky to find trees half that size in this part of the province.

The trail was relatively clear, probably kept open by ranchers for quick access to their roaming livestock. We took several different turns, ever decreasing in elevation with a deep gully on our left, which eventually turned into a ravine. Jud mentioned there was once a small settlement in the area named Criss but we were unable to find its exact location. Eventually we emerged beside a rancher's outbuilding; the owner returned our waves with obvious amusement as we passed through his yard onto the main road. At the Seven Lakes junction Jud turned through an open gate into some old trails again. From here, after numerous twists and turns, we found ourselves on the Sebastion FSR. Now I consider myself blessed with an above average sense of direction, but after following Jud for the last several hours I was thoroughly disoriented. It was difficult enough just to keep Jud's rear bumper in sight to avoid becoming separated or lost. There was no way I would have been able to retrace our steps.

Eventually we joined the Criss Creek Main. After crossing the Criss Creek Bridge we traversed the north side of the valley high up on a shelf road. This creek was worked by Chinese placer miners years ago. From our lofty position we could see no signs of any tailings or other workings. That would have to wait for a future trip, naturally with gold pans in hand.

Split Rock

Just before the descent into the Deadman Valley we passed 'Split Rock', a huge cliff face that appears as though severed by a giant's meat cleaver. Local legend indicates that an old trail, dating back to the fur trading days of the early 1800s, passed through this rock. Perhaps the doomed North West Fur Company employee and his ill-tempered companion had traversed this very cut, en-route to the trading post at Vidette Lake. It was too late in the day to scramble up the slope and explore the steep ravine. We added it to the list for our next visit.

We emerged back onto the Deadman Valley Road from Criss Creek Main, our trucks dusty and fuel tanks near empty, and knew our exploration of this beautiful area had ended.

We followed Jud back to Savona, filled up our trucks at the gas station, and treated ourselves to an ice cream. We sat in the shade of Jud's truck and watched the busyness of the highway. We had not seen traffic for the past two days and we were overwhelmed by all the movement and noise. I longed for our quiet camp spot at Fatox Lake.

The daylight dwindled and forced us to our feet. We confirmed our list of future 'to dos' for our next visit to Deadman Valley with Jud. Hopefully our follow-up trip would not take as many years to embark upon as my first trip.

In Reflection...

Contrary to its ominous sounding name Deadman Valley and its surroundings openly shared an abundance of life with us. Any child or adult who loves the outdoors will find the colourful variety of flora and fauna, numerous clear valley lakes and many landscape marvels within the Deadman are like Nature's never-ending art, and much of it accessible by the family sedan. Our brief two-day backroad excursion nurtured my soul. I returned home feeling calm and invigorated, a long-held curiosity finally satiated.

Meanwhile, back at the dusty signpost for the Deadman Vidette Road on Highway 1, the traffic continues to whiz past, everyone en-route to a predetermined destination for a predetermined time, too busy to stop and explore the Deadman Valley secrets.

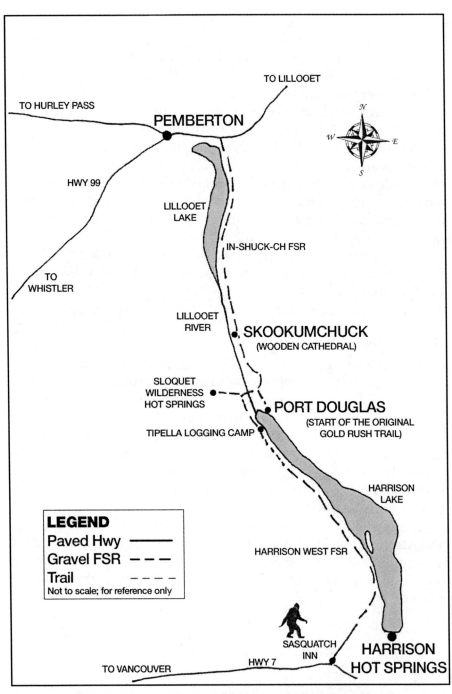

TO LILLOOET

TO HURLEY PASS

PEMBERTON

HWY 99

LILLOOET LAKE

IN-SHUCK-CH FSR

TO WHISTLER

LILLOOET RIVER

SKOOKUMCHUCK
(WOODEN CATHEDRAL)

SLOQUET WILDERNESS HOT SPRINGS

PORT DOUGLAS
(START OF THE ORIGINAL GOLD RUSH TRAIL)

TIPELLA LOGGING CAMP

HARRISON LAKE

LEGEND
Paved Hwy ———
Gravel FSR – – –
Trail - - - -
Not to scale; for reference only

HARRISON WEST FSR

SASQUATCH INN

TO VANCOUVER   HWY 7

HARRISON HOT SPRINGS

HARRISON WEST TRAVERSE - HWY 7 TO HWY 99

Gold Traces, Golden Spaces

... we lingered, capturing the synergy of this first modern gateway to the interior of BC over which so many determined men had travelled to seek their fortune. We left quietly so as not to disturb the spirits of long ago.

In the Beginning...

I had planned this outing since the dead of winter, when the mountain trails of BC find themselves more snow-covered and more impassable every day, and Christmas camping gifts lay idle waiting, along with their owners, for the promise of spring and the call of duty for a new backroad adventure. Many long dark evenings were spent scouring maps and history books; minds busy, spirits restless. Finally the sun's endless cycle again initiated the change of seasons and our camping gear emerged from its long hibernation.

This backroad journey would see us explore the west side of Harrison Lake to a hot spring tucked deep into the towering coastal mountains. We would visit the Douglas Trail, stop at a century old cathedral built by Natives, cross the Hurley Pass to ghost towns in the Gold Bridge Valley, and spend a night in an abandoned prospector's cabin in the Yalakom River Valley. I had never ventured past the Harrison Lake area. It promised to be a week filled with history and adventure.

On the Trail... Harrison Lake to Pemberton

We were parked at the Sasquatch Inn on Highway 7. It was mid-morning and we stopped for an early lunch. Over the years the parking lot of this infamous tavern, now half a century young, was the meeting point for many a Vancouver based four-wheel drive club for adventures into the beautiful Harrison Valley backcountry. We had an entire week after the May long weekend. We aired down and headed north on the West Harrison FSR.

The West Harrison logging road follows the shiny hydro-power transmission lines as they leap in enormous swoops from one high point to the next. This feat of progress winds up the west side of Harrison Lake for about eighty kilometres before it reaches the Lillooet River. At this point the backroad and transmission lines cross the river and continue past the village of Skookumchuk, up the east side of Lillooet Lake, eventually reaching Duffy Lake Road near Pemberton. Strictly speaking the majority of this route does not require four-wheel drive, just an adventurous spirit and a vehicle with sufficient ground clearance. However, its length and washboard roughness will make it exhausting if attempted in a single day. This backroad has opened up a valley of outstanding scenic beauty, long lakes, steep mountains, rushing creeks and never-ending flora.

An hour into our journey, along a blind corner, we came across a young couple in a stranded vehicle. We stopped and they asked us if we happened to have a tire patch kit. Their truck had a flat, and with no key for their locking wheel nut they could not remove the tire and replace it with their spare. The driver did have a small pump. However, the hole in the tire was too large, and the air pump could not keep sufficient pressure in the tire to drive on.

At the time I did not carry a patch kit (though I do now). I tried various tricks with the tools I carried to loosen the one locking nut but to no avail. Frustrated I eventually gave up. The couple's friends had departed for home, a country away in Washington State, with instructions to locate the missing key for the locking wheel nut. Unfortunately they would not be back for many hours. I am sure that driver would never leave on another backroad trip without the proper key for his rims. Some lessons are learned the hard way. We bid them good luck and left them awaiting their friends' arrival.

Karen made a comment on some beautiful white flowering trees. They were Pacific Dogwood, British Columbia's floral emblem. This plant can grow up to seventy feet high and is protected by law in BC. Each flower has four to six white petals. However, in reality each 'flower' is a group of tiny flowers

Dogwood, BC's floral emblem

inside the large white petals, known as bracts. Inside the bracts are up to twenty small greenish flowers. Dogwood was used by early Natives for wooden handles, hooks and anything else that required the use of a hard wood.

We stopped to take pictures and waded through waist high snapdragons and orange tiger lilies along the roadside. A myriad of scents engulfed us. A redheaded woodpecker came to investigate, nervously flying from tree to tree. The splendid bird was at first upset, and then when satisfied that we were not competing for its breakfast, resumed picking bugs from a grove

33

of ancient cedars above us.

The road became roller-coaster like, designed for access not for speed. The road's edge was at times near the water, at other times the water was incredibly far below. Our constant companions were soaring peaks, snow crowned and bold, always visible to the east and when the valley widened sufficiently, to the west as well. This was west coast backroad scenery at its best.

Several hours later at Bremner Creek, the road dwindled and the rough and steep sections started. A high clearance vehicle was a necessity and four-wheel drive an asset. My last trip down this trail was six years previous, at which time the numerous creeks were crossed by old 'tree bridges', narrow and exciting. Gigantic Western Red cedars had been felled, who knows how long ago, then four or five of the trunks were placed across the creek and bound together with steel cables. Rough hewn planks completed the decking and impassable creek canyons were suddenly passable. I enjoyed the site of these old wooden bridges, portraying man's ingenuity and the use of natural resources in their rawest form. These bridges of yesterday were now replaced by reinforced foundations, large steel girders and expertly placed cement deck plates. On the positive side the responsible authorities replaced the bridges after ripping out the old ones. I have come to many creek crossings in other backcountry areas where the old bridges have been unceremoniously removed and not replaced, making passage impossible to favourite trails.

At the 80km marker we drove through the Tipella logging operation. Here, on several acres of wasteland, lay gigantic piles of freshly logged trees for transport by tugboat to the insatiable sawmills south of the lake. Turn-of-the-century maps list a town site called Tipella in this area. It was owned by the Fire Mountain Gold Mining Company, which commenced a mining operation on nearby Fire Mountain in 1898. It was optimistically called 'The Money Spinner'. Large gold finds never materialised and the town of Tipella, along with the mine, were soon abandoned. Now, many years later, the old growth trees of Fire Mountain are turned into someone's fortune.

The trail at this point changed its name to the Lillooet FSR and became two-wheel drive again. It was now late afternoon. Several kilometres later we crossed the Sloquet Creek Bridge and we turned left to the Sloquet Hot Springs, our night's destination.

After we turned off the Main, a lynx sprang out of the underbrush in front of us. This rarely-seen feline trotted merrily ahead of our vehicle, acting oblivious to our presence. I fumbled with the camera as I drove and eventually managed to snap a picture of its right rear leg as it disappeared into the bush. My emotions on that photo opportunity could be summed up in two words: substantially frustrated.

We found our way to the springs, nestled in a steep mountain valley. The last of the weekend campers were packing up to leave. This left the springs entirely deserted. Sloquet Hot Springs is a long drive from Vancouver and that is not necessarily a bad thing. Considering that this is not an official campground or Forest Recreation Site, people need to be diligent to pack out what they pack in. (Note: at the time of publication of this book this area is now a Forest Recreation Site requiring payment for use and provides picnic benches and outhouse facilities.)

After setting up camp we took the steep trail to the undeveloped hot spring, a ten-minute walk from our site. The hot spring was divided by natural rock walls into separate pools, ranging from very hot, to medium warm, to ice cold, if one included the nearby glacier-fed Sloquet Creek. Numerous people had obviously donated time and energy ensuring safe access to the pools for the benefit of all visitors.

Soaking in Mother Earth's healing waters was an immediate and powerful connection to Nature. Karen and I lavished in the natural cradle. Our dog Keera flopped down beside the pools. As she dozed her nose twitched with every tiny breeze, the spring's slight sulphur vapours overpowering her delicate sense of smell. The roar of the nearby Sloquet Creek, thundering down from the steep surrounding mountains, was muffled

Sloquet's natural hot springs

by the steam of the springs swirling around us, delicately coating everything within its reach. We felt like we had our own private five star Jacuzzi suite, complete with water plants and exotic birds... well, finches and humming birds anyway. This was a place to cherish and honour, truly a golden space on earth.

We alternated several times between the bone-chilling creek and the hot pools, and were almost too relaxed to struggle back to camp for dinner. That evening, under the forest's enormous cedar canopy, the evening-mist hung deep, mingling with our camp smoke. When the fire died, the Sloquet shadows took their final possession of our secluded camp. Spent, we crept into our tent leaving the night to the vastness of the mountains. We slept deeply.

We awoke to drizzle and cooler temperatures. No problem; we knew where to get warm, even hot if required. After breakfast, with towels in hand, we hiked down to the springs and soaked the morning away. On our return to camp, we may as well have been conquering Mount Everest. Our legs felt like rubber as we laboured up the hill to our campsite. After lunch we treated ourselves to a nap and woke up just in time for dinner. Then it was back to the springs for a candle-lit soak. Entranced by the deepest relaxation I had felt in recent memory we found ourselves back in our sleeping bags. This was Nature's spa retreat at its finest.

The Forestry bridge over Lillooet River

The next morning we noticed another vehicle had arrived during the night. As we now felt 'crowded', and had plans to meet up with our camping friends Kari and Lucy on the next leg of our backroad adventure, we bid our quiet paradise good-bye and packed up the Toyota.

If you do make the journey to visit this golden space please carry out more garbage than you bring in. Help ensure that this natural setting will be open for all to enjoy for a long time.

Once back on the Main we took the bridge over the Lillooet River. Heading north, insignificant-looking markers indicated the Douglas Heritage Trail. This long forgotten road is named after a bold and large figure in BC's history: the Scotsman James Douglas. An employee of the powerful fur trading Hudson's Bay Company (HBC), Douglas rose through the ranks to take the Director position of its vast western operations in the late 1840s.

The last standing cabin on the Douglas Trail

Large deposits of placer gold were discovered in the interior of BC and American gold seekers started to pour into the sparsely populated colony of New Caledonia in early 1858.

Douglas knew major changes were inevitable, and not necessarily favourable for the British colony. As the pick-axe totting men continued their march across the 49th parallel, Douglas proved as astute in politics as he had been in collecting furs.

He tirelessly lobbied the lawmakers in far-off Great Britain to create a new colony, to supply capital, human resources and enforce British law before American-style lawlessness found its way north and the area's vast resources disappeared south. The power brokers in Britain had other concerns than the destiny of the distant and apparently unimportant colony full of impossible-to-cross mountains somewhere by the Pacific. After all, other than an over-abundance of fur bearing animals with two large front teeth and towering spruce trees for use as masts in Her Majesty's Navy, it was of little value.

Or was it? In November of 1858 the HBC Director's persistence paid off and he became the first Governor of British Columbia, several months after the Province itself was proclaimed and thus named by Queen Victoria of England. Douglas steered the province through its infancy, a period of tremendous growth and challenge. He laid the foundation for BC to emerge as a world producer of resources and attain its enviable standard of living. At a time when American interests were constantly talking of annexation he can be credited with keeping British Columbia in Canada before either formally existed. Douglas spearheaded many ambitious construction projects starting with the building of the first road into the BC interior; the Douglas Trail, which was replaced in 1864 by the 'impossible to build' route through the Fraser Canyon.

In the summer of 1858 thousands of idle prospectors were squatting on the many sand bars along the mouth of the Fraser River waiting out the winter runoff. As these men restlessly whispered the 'word' in languages from around the globe they loafed and brooded, waiting to make their way up the treacherous river into the promised land full of gold but devoid of roads. Douglas proposed to hire some of these men to build an access road into the interior. Five hundred prospectors agreed to pick up axes and hack a road out of the primeval forest. The following year the Royal Engineers, sent out from England, widened the trail into full road status. Yes, this is the granddaddy of all BC interior roads and highways. This road has carried thousands of prospectors, packers mule teams, ox wagons and even camels into the gold fields of the upper Fraser and the Caribou. It runs from Port Douglas, named after James, on the north end of Harrison Lake to Lillooet, then named Cayoosh, via Lillooet Lake, Birkenhead River, Seton Lake and Anderson Lake. All these waterways were traversed by steamers. In Lillooet it connected to Mile 0 of the Caribou Gold Rush Trail.

Curious to sample the historic spell of this obscure and now un-travelled route, we hiked several crooked kilometres of the moss covered Douglas Trail with not a tire tread in sight. Despite overgrown sections and wash-outs, it was in remarkable condition considering its age and crude means of construction. In pouring rain we arrived at our destination, the final remaining roadhouse. Three weathered cabins in varying condition from 'demolished' to 'almost salvageable' were surrounded, or in some cases overgrown, by the lush rain forest.

Lengths of old corral fencing lay on the ground, a distinct rotting line, undisturbed by human hands for decades. The corral now only held mature conifers, no evidence of horses or oxen remained. Rusted machinery parts lay about, signs of 'modern' passers-by. We lingered, capturing the synergy of this first modern gateway to the interior of BC over which so many determined men had travelled to seek their fortune. We left quietly so as not to disturb the spirits of long ago.

Our next stop was the century old wooden cathedral overlooking the Native village of Skookumchuck. The word 'skookumchuk' is Native for 'turbulent river'. The steepled Church of the Holy Cross was built in 1905 by Native artisans under the direction of the Oblate Fathers. At the nearby cemetery we discovered ornately decorated headstones, some weeks old, others dated from the 1890s. Apparently they still held services here. Despite its prominent location in the village, the church languished in desperate disrepair, as did most of the village homes. Its outer skin peeled and broken, it stood as a wistful foreground to the supporting steel lines that carried hydro power to Vancouver's affluent suburbs not so far away.

We returned to our trucks and continued north to visit sev-

40

eral Native family burial plots adjacent to the road. The road along Lillooet Lake continued through park-like country. Oncoming traffic consisted mainly of fishermen, towing their faithful motorboats. Perhaps they were headed for the numerous camp sites dotting the lakeshore, the occupied ones betrayed

Century old wooden cathedral in Skookumchuk

by a puff of wood smoke. Several hours later we exited onto the pavement at Duffy Lake Road and turned left into Pemberton. The truck's trip odometer read 213 new kilometres – it seemed we had gone much further.

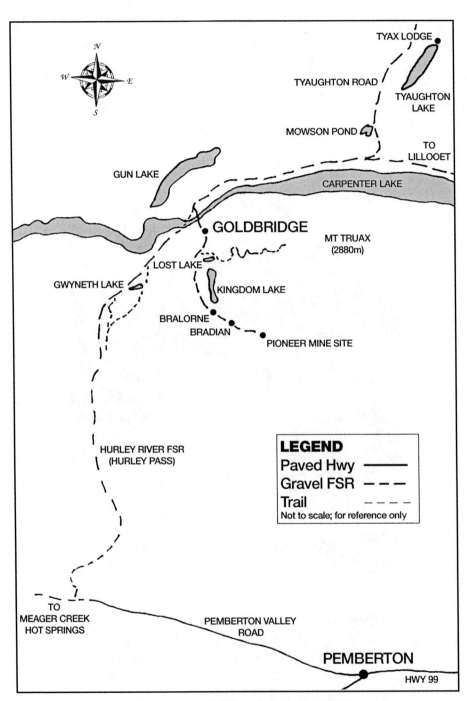

HURLEY PASS TO GOLD BRIDGE

...Pemberton to Gold Bridge Valley

The town of Pemberton is named after Joseph Pemberton. Employed by the HBC during the 1850s and 1860s as Surveyor General, Pemberton drew up the first surveys of the area.

Pemberton is described in his daughter's memoir as 'cheery, bright and of a most amiable nature', and the town of Pemberton appeared to radiate the qualities of its namesake. After a visit to several businesses, which included the local deli, we parked in an open lot, set up our camping chairs and relaxed with a plate of hot food. The residents that passed by smiled at us; some stopped to talk. The local RCMP cruiser went by; the constable smiled and gave a warm wave. Pemberton made us feel at home.

We followed the pavement west of town until we hit gravel and turned at the Hurley Pass FSR sign. The Hurley Pass was built by logging companies in the 1970s to tap into the vast logging reserves in the Carpenter Lake area. Every May long weekend the mountain pass is painstakingly cleared of snow to allow passage into the area without having to travel the long way through Lillooet.

The Hurley route provided generous views of the Pemberton valley on its way up the south slopes. The pass was wide, rough and worn; typical for a heavily used logging road. As we crested the summit the towering snow banks imparted a roofless tunnel effect, as if driving down an Olympic loge ride. The bulldozer had chewed through fifteen feet of snow at the summit that year, not a small task.

With our camping gear still wet from the night before we decided to treat ourselves to the Tyax Lodge on beautiful Tyaughton Lake. We arrived at nightfall. We were to meet our camping companions the next day at a nearby camp site.

Tyax Lodge is a year round resort. It was built in 1986 of logs from the land it sits on. Despite its many upscale services it still maintains a friendly log cabin charm.

The resort had few guests and we soaked in the silence that hung throughout the lodge timbers.

Hurley Pass snowbanks in May

Late the next morning we made our way to the nearby camping sites at Mowson Pond. As we set up camp Kari, Lucy and their German Shepherd, Sprocket, arrived. Our dogs instantly broke into enthusiastic play, competing for top dust-raising honours. After lunch we were all eager to explore the surrounding mountains and valleys. Our exhausted dogs were grateful for the rest.

The Bridge River Valley area includes what is now known as Gold Bridge, Bralorne, Carpenter Lake, Gun Lake and Tyaughton Lake. Before the introduction of Europeans, nomadic Chilcotin and Lillooet tribes would frequent the area to forage and hunt. When white prospectors first discovered gold in 1858 the Natives attempted to resist the intrusion. Purportedly a great Chief called Hunter Jack had his own gold mines and guarded his cache with his life.

After his death, many went out to find his secret source but to no avail. However, rich gold deposits were discovered on many of the rivers including the Cadwallader, Noel and Hurley Rivers. In the 1920s the famed Pioneer and Gold Bridge mines started production deep inside the surrounding mountains. Well funded companies chased gold veins to extraordinary depths. By the time they ceased operation in the 1960s they had produced $145 million worth of bullion. During the peak production years over 5000 people worked in the area and enjoyed services as varied as a hospital, bank, ski hill, skating rink, stores,

Tyax Lodge on Tyaughton Lake

outdoor pool, schools and hotels. We made several of these places our destination for the day.

Our first stop was for fuel and supplies in Gold Bridge. As alcohol, gambling and women of questionable character were not allowed in the main company town of Bralorne, Gold Bridge

45

Welcome to Gold Bridge

was born some distance away. Today, this town is blessed with a population of 43 souls, (as proudly proclaimed by the town welcome sign) and has one store and one gas pump.

After filling our fuel tanks we strolled around the hamlet past the former bakery, hotel and motel, false fronted general store and back to the gas pump shack: a town of 43 inhabitants is obviously not too big. Yet, despite its size, this one-time red light district is now the centre of commerce for the entire Bridge River Valley.

We drove up the steep gravel access road to Bralorne, tucked deep into a side valley. Tiny Bralorne evoked memories of a close-knit community and an easier-going time, when company towns were flush with cash and its inhabitants were happily isolated from the outside world. Bralorne was an eclectic mix of buildings from picturesque decay to newly renovated. With rumours of the Bralorne Mine re-opening and real estate values far below those of settlements to the south of Hurley Pass the local talk was abuzz with potential newcomers to this delightful region. Thankfully, the 'boom' word was still absent, and the quiet and peaceful atmosphere and feeling of remoteness would for the time being remain over the area.

Gold Bridge General Store

Several kilometres along Cadwallader Creek we arrived at the abandoned Pioneer Mine site. We parked at the bridge by the creek and explored on foot. The mill building had completely collapsed; the heavy snows of the area had turned it into a large pile of bleaching debris. On higher ground the skeleton of the crusher building sat in quiet resignation, its walls damaged, its doors and windows completely missing. It waited for the hand of fate to end its slow demise. The building's crushers, with the manufacturer's inscription 'Allentown USA' still clearly legible, sat quiet for nearly half a century. During operations this building would have been the noisiest part of the mining site, with the pounding of machinery echoing throughout the forest.

Cautiously, we climbed the outdoor stairwell to the company homes. The stairwell was in amazing condition and ended at a plateau above the crusher building. We hiked down the

Pioneer homes, now quiet

grown-in trails to the former residence sites. Dedicated men once lived here with their wives and children, spurred on by ambition and faith to meet the challenges of hard rock mining.

It was tough, dangerous work but for many, especially during the Great Depression, it was a wonderful place to call home. Looking and listening, it was easy to envision the neatly trimmed gardens and white picket fences that once adorned the streets of this small suburb. The fancy homes featured the most modern of amenities for their time: electricity, plumbing, full bathrooms and basements. The homes now ranged from totally ruined, to salvageable.

We walked past the dark and hollow homes that yesterday reverberated with human spirit and laughter. A light mist settled in, drifting down the weed covered streets and around Pioneer's relics. The abandoned town site slowly turned into an Armageddon movie back drop, sure to quicken any Hollywood producer's pulse. Amazing how the simple passage of time can effect such changes.

On our way back to camp Kari took us on a detour. On a previous trip he had navigated a trail to a difficult creek crossing. He decided to wait for a backup vehicle before attempting the ford. According to our maps the trail led to an old mine high in the Truax range.

We arrived at the creek bank and got out to survey the challenge. The creek crossing was not exceptionally deep or wide but a cow-size boulder and a large log in the middle of the crossing presented quite an obstacle. The near bank would be a steep slide with little room to navigate around the boulder and log. The far bank was even steeper and covered with thick mud and required an immediate hard turn to the left once the front wheels reached the top of the embankment.

Kari nudged the 4Runner into low and inched down the bank. His rig's custom suspension allowed him to traverse the off-camber section with minimal body roll. As soon as his front wheels found water he turned towards the boulder. He kept close to the boulder to line himself up as perpendicular as possible with the far bank. To achieve this, Kari repeatedly backed up a few feet and then drove forward a few feet to get the 4Runner's rear-end within inches of the boulder. As usual, Kari's twenty-plus years of off-road experience made it all look easy and almost rehearsed.

Once he was as straight as the boulder would allow him, he charged for the mud and hoped his speed would carry him through. It took several attempts for his mud tires to find sufficient grip. Finally the 4Runner found itself on solid footing.

Then it was my turn. I took a final look at the crude ford, its natural obstacles and the steep embankment on the far side. I repeatedly envisioned the route I would take and climbed into our truck. Karen and Keera had made their way across the log to the other side and were waiting with Kari and Lucy. I engaged the rear locker and slipped into low gear. I felt my front driver side tire drop lower and lower and lower still. I was shooting to swing wider than Kari had driven, thereby increasing my off-camber angle but also reducing the number of backups

Creek ford near Lost Lake

required. The creek bed was hard and firm but I did not want to disturb it any more than necessary. I crawled ahead by several feet while the truck's off-camber angle, and consequentially my anxiety, reached an alarming level. I had underestimated the steepness of the bank - I quickly realised I should have followed Kari's line. But, despite the short distance driven, I was far beyond the point of backing up. I felt panic. The tighter I grabbed the wheel, the worse my tension became. The Toyota's suspension creaked and groaned, protesting its push to the limit. The truck chassis continued to faithfully follow gravity. Finally, the front passenger tire started to descend the bank, instantly reducing the truck's tipping potential. My grip released and I took a deep breath. I had cut the angle so tight that no back-ups were required in the creek. The front locker in my truck is seldom used but I engaged it before powering up the far bank. With the hood pointed skyward and the rear bumper under water, my front mud tires fought for traction on the steep incline. I was up in the first attempt. Sitting level again I disengaged the lockers and with a big grin, greeted Karen as she climbed into the cab.

We stopped at an abandoned Forest Recreation Site at a lake appropriately named Lost Lake and climbed out to admire the scenery. Located at the base of the towering mountains the mood of the day was caught in its shimmer. Large aquatic plants followed its shoreline and a mother mallard mustered her brood through tall grasses, all the while watchful of a predator whose huge nest and squawking offspring hung in the uppermost branches of a nearby tree. On shore, rotting firewood neatly stacked, decaying picnic benches, and fire pits covered in twigs and pine needles patiently awaited us. At some point in the past the creek crossing became too challenging for most and this kingdom fell exclusively to the original inhabitants of this hinterland. What a beautiful place to catch a daybreak and then laze it away.

The trail became extremely overgrown. The alder brush punished our paint finish with deep scratches and scrapes, daring us to continue. Up ahead, out of sight, I could hear Kari's chainsaw ripping through the deadfall that littered this obscure route through the forest. The trail wasted no time gaining elevation with switchback after switchback. No real estate wasted here. This was typical of early mining roads.

We came to a large deadfall which required both our chainsaws to buck it up. Karen and Lucy joined in with machetes to clear the smaller branches and bushes. Even Sprocket and Keera helped, gnawing and chewing on the smaller wooden trail debris until only a few minuscule remains were coughed out. For an hour we toiled to clear the way. Of course Mother

The reflection of Lost Lake

Nature decided it was time to water her garden and mix it up with intermittent hail stones. With sweat pouring down my temples, hands throbbing from the chainsaw and sore back muscles I straightened up and gazed at the snow covered mountains around us. Truax Mountain resembled the evil castle from

'The Two Towers' movie trilogy. I fantasized about Troll warriors flooding towards us, ready to annihilate anything in their way. Perhaps they could help us clear the deadfall. To the west, low pressure clouds parted and lifted around the peaks. The rains cooled my skin and steam rose from my damp clothes as if on fire. For a mountain lover like me this was truly a golden space.

As the rain let up we had the trail clear. We savoured a drink from the nearby creek, climbed into our vehicles and carried on. Soon the switchbacks became so tight they required two and three point turns. At one such turn I noticed a small cut at the end of the switchback. This was the first turn-around opportunity on the entire trail. I suggested on the CB that we park and explore further on foot. Kari and Lucy agreed.

Lucy stayed with the trucks, while the rest of us proceeded on foot. We had not gone far when we came across a deep washout. This would require several hours of reconstruction to pass by vehicle. It was too late in the day for this type of trail activity. We hoped we were close to the mine and continued by foot.

With high altitude winds slicing through our damp clothes we quickened our pace. The rocky track led ever higher. Sweating and tired, we broke into a breathtaking gorge just as the trail levelled and entered the rear of the mountain face. We were greeted by the wildest of landscapes... to our left, reaching hundreds of metres above us, was a half-bowl basin completely devoid of plant life. Starring down on us from the ridgeline were countless jagged spires. At the base, lichen-covered boulders, many car-size and larger, appeared as toys tossed about by an ill-tempered giant. Half-way up the basin only layered shale managed to cling to the steep slopes: more Two Tower fantasies swirled through my mind. How small I felt. To our right dribbled icy streams of the purest water. They disappeared into the forest edge, seeking to join the tumbling echoes of the creek far below us. The trail veered sharply to the right and, as it continued into deep timber shadows, was covered by several feet of snow. Karen and Keera decided to wait while Kari, Sprocket and I continued. With every other step I broke through the snow's crust and sunk knee deep. I too stopped after a short distance. Kari and Sprocket were too determined to let a little snow end their search for the elusive mine. I lost sight of man and dog as they rounded the next corner.

I made my way back to Karen and we hugged to stay warm. Surrounded by the rawness of Nature we tried our best to ignore the biting gusts. Keera lay sphinx-like on the snow facing the rocky bowl, scouring the heights with keen observance. Even she seemed impressed.

After a long while Kari returned, with Sprocket struggling through his master's deep snow prints, a look of disappointment on their faces. We turned to start our escape from the cold winds. With one last glance I left behind the magic of this natural hide-out that so stirred my imagination. Who knew when the next adventurer would feast on these surroundings?

Once we had the rigs turned around we crawled down the switchbacks, the bush punishing our vehicle paint anew. We crossed back over the creek where it was my turn to get hung up. Even with lockers, if you pick the wrong line things can be tricky. After a number of attempts I finally found firm soil on the far embankment. We drifted through Gold Bridge and back to camp for dinner around the fire.

After dinner a member of the Tyax Lodge staff stopped by to warn us that grizzlies with cubs were roaming the area. We kept our dogs inside our trucks but all night long they sounded the canine alarms bells. Perhaps the grizzlies were close.

The next morning we rose late. We made our way to Gwyneth Lake and followed an old trail down to the Hurley River. The trail was in good shape and had been cleared a few years earlier. There were no difficult sections other than steep downhill grades as we made our way to the river valley. This trail was like a paved freeway compared to yesterday's grown-in mountain trek.

We arrived at another abandoned Forest Recreation Site where the trail abruptly ended at a huge washout. A lookout platform, complete with a lovingly built and decorated bench, was perched above the river: the perfect spot to sit in the wilderness and contemplate life.

After a late tailgate lunch we took a different trail which followed along the shore of the Hurley River. Everywhere were

The Hurley Chair Cabin

signs of mining activity: moss covered bridge remnants, rusting machinery caught between grasses, and miles of wooden water flumes broken along the river banks.

We stopped at an old cabin which, judging by the build style, was only half a century old. We pushed the door open and were greeted by a peculiar and eerie sight. The cabin was totally

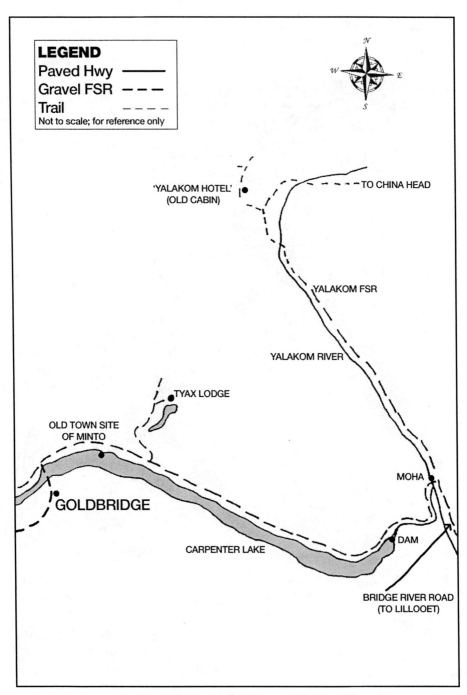

GOLD BRIDGE TO YALAKOM RIVER

deserted, save one old tattered but ornately carved armchair. It would have been an expensive and beautiful piece of furniture when new. It was in the middle of the little cabin facing the doorway, as if guarding the cabin's entrance and awaiting the return of its rightful owner. We half expected that at any moment he would come home from his gold workings and sit down in 'his' chair.

As our trucks rolled again the trail became more aggressive; mud, washouts and precipitous drop-offs required precise navigation often with only inches to spare.

Eventually the trail started to gain in elevation and led us up and away from the river valley. After several hours we exited onto the Hurley Main. We returned to camp for an early dinner. The dogs were quiet that night; the grizzlies must have moved on.

...Gold Bridge to Yalakom River

The next morning we broke camp to head for our final destination, the Yalakom River Valley. The fifty-five kilometre backroad along the vertical edge of Carpenter Lake was winding, slow, and beautiful. Mountains rose sharply from the shores and deep side-canyons carved by runoff waters offered hidden waterfalls and wildlife sightings to those that take the time to notice.

We passed the Terzaghi Dam into the Bridge River Canyon. Government surveyors and road builders once considered this canyon inaccessible. However, a group of local prospectors rose to the challenge. Armed with determination and high explosives they blasted and undercut the vertical cliff walls; the canyon was accessible after all. Since the building of the dam the only water in Bridge River comes from a few creeks below the dam leaving the river almost dry at certain times of the year.

The Yalakom River met the Bridge River in a torrent of foam; the road veered. A short steep climb later we crested the canyon benches, leaving the green and forested hills of the

Carpenter Lake - a slow and beautiful drive

Bridge River Valley behind. Here, widely spaced pines seared in the heat of the large semi-arid valley. Through the eons the Yalakom River has cut through immense beds of gravel and now snakes far below the canyon rim.

At the Y-intersection near Moha we turned north up the Yalakom Main. With a name like Yalakom I expected adventure. The route did not disappoint. The Yalakom Main is not a tough four-wheel drive trek but it is not to be taken lightly. Starting at the Y-intersection the road's smooth almost pavement-like dirt surface eventually turned into a narrow trail with amazingly steep drop-offs, and was often strewn with rocks and boulders loosened by the high winds known to frequent this long valley. One boulder we carefully navigated around would necessitate the use of heavy equipment to remove. On one curve we encountered a pair of white knuckled drivers proceeding v-e-r-y slowly. They were obviously respectful of the consequences of not paying attention on the countless unguarded cliff sections. Pockets of fences in disrepair and old log buildings weathered to the colour of the surrounding rock came into view.

Driving through Bridge River Gorge

We took a side trail that led to an abandoned mine. As we approached the sub-alpine deep snow drifts obliged us to turn around. Numerous other bumpy and water-soaked side routes dealt us the same hand; time after time we reached a point

The Yalakom River, far below

where the high-elevation snows forced our retreat. These trails would not be passable for several months. We stuck to the gravelled Main, and followed the Yalakom Road for several hours before driving off the coverage area of my map book. Kari had driven this route previously so all eyes would follow him. Eventually we neared the end of the valley and the Main itself turned into a rough track as we were forced into the higher elevations again.

Evergreen aromas now replaced the savour of sage and juniper scents. Kari and Lucy became high-centred in a large snowdrift. After attempting to dig the vehicle out with long handled shovels, we resorted to Kari's winch. We pulled him through the drift, carefully turned him around on the narrow slippery trail, and helped him back down to where I had already parked before the snow drift. The sun had disappeared behind the mountains. With dusk approaching our energy levels fell as fast as the alpine temperatures. We considered setting up our tents on the trail, but decided to investigate a dilapidated log cabin we noticed several kilometres back, a short

The 'Yalakom Hotel'

distance from the trail. After parking as close as possible, we walked the rest of the distance.

With a critical eye we examined the forlorn abode. Granted, the shelter sat in a fairy-tale setting, located on a small rise overlooking a greening meadow with large firs hiding it from prying views. A small brook followed the narrow valley and blessed the area with a carefree aura. Icicles hung from the neglected sod-covered roof which had loose and missing sections. The dull grey cabin logs had been placed long ago by experienced hands with attention to detail. A single rusty stovepipe reached through the roof and the small windows, though

61

yellowed by age and dust, were all intact. The tiny covered veranda, littered with tree debris, creaked as we stepped up. A primitive table built of tree branches stood unused in the corner, deer antlers piled underneath.

Uncertain, we first knocked and then opened the door. We entered the single-room cabin. Inside, a pleasant fragrance of wood smoke and hearty foods enveloped us. The smell of rodents so often prevalent in abandoned buildings in the wilderness was totally absent. In fact, in complete contrast to the cabin's exterior, the interior was clean and felt inviting. The floor was swept, candles were neatly placed on a small table in the centre of the room, and wooden bed frames occupied two walls. Standing guard beside the single doorway, a home-made corn broom obliged all occupants to clean up after themselves before leaving. The deluxe feature to our night's accommodation was that the room had a fully functional wood stove, custom crafted from a rusty fuel drum. This cabin would keep us snug and warm, as it surely had for others, during the cold mountain night. Feeling exceptionally blessed for our good fortune we set up camp. Kari and I cut and hauled firewood for the evening, while Lucy and Karen prepped the cabin and cooked dinner. Keera and Sprocket, restless from the day's inactivity in the back of the trucks, were rustling bushes in the distance.

That night we relaxed around the wood stove, its loading door half open, an orange glow spilling across the cabin and into our hearts. We felt wonderfully warm and content. Despite our long day we stayed up for many hours, speculating and theorising about the 'Yalakom Hotel' as we called the cabin. How many oceans and lands had the original builder crossed? What was his name? When was it built? Who was tending the cabin now?

Finally, one by one, we fell silent; we had nothing more to add, nothing more to ask. Maybe we were just too tired. After satisfying ourselves one more time that the cabin was indeed rodent proof we crawled into our sleeping bags and drifted off.

After breakfast the next morning we explored the surrounding area. There was a rotten wood foundation imbedded in the creek. Perhaps the original builder had engineering skills proficient enough to generate his own power with the help of a water wheel - or was it a means of anchoring a crude sluice? We found an old mine shaft not far away. It had collapsed within a few feet of the entrance. Likely there were other shafts in the vicinity of the cabin to be discovered though we found no more.

With one last whisk of the corn broom, we stepped out and secured the door of the Yalakom Hotel. We turned our vehicles around and I took a long final look. In one night I had grown very fond of the old log building and tiny valley; the atmosphere of tranquility ranked it near the top of golden spaces on our trip.

We followed our tracks from yesterday, along the Yalakom River, all the way back to the Bridge River Road, and eventually to the historic town of Lillooet. We filled up our empty fuel tanks and aired up our tires for the pavement trip home.

After spending a week in the mountain wilderness, we found the hustle and bustle of 'downtown Lillooet' overwhelming. We bid our good-byes to Kari, Lucy and Sprocket. Both trucks quickly hit the open highway, destined in opposite directions.

In Reflection...

The gold mining industry in BC established the modern history of the province. Many highways and towns that exist today are a result of gold trails and gold mines that existed yesterday. Together they laid the initial cornerstone to British Columbia's prosperity and a way of life for generations.

For those willing to travel off the beaten track the relics of the province's impressive gold mining history await discovery. And, make sure to take the time to explore the countless golden spaces found along the way.

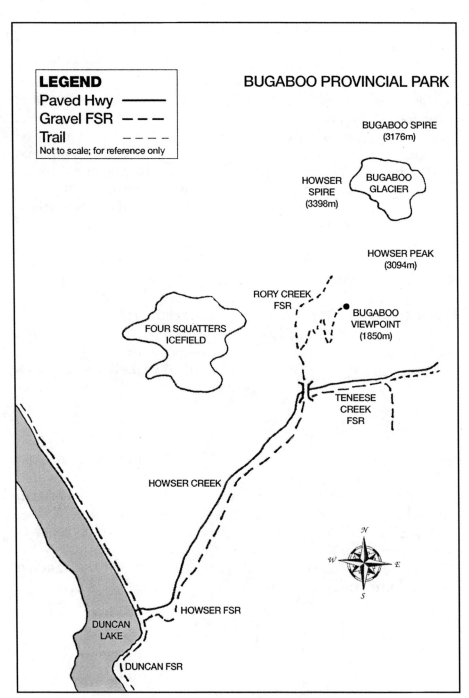

HOWSER - BUGABOO VIEWPOINT TRAIL

A Peek in the Bugaboos

And there it stood. Tall, big...simply majestic, no other word was fitting.

In the Beginning...

Millions of years ago, not long in geological time, winds howled across barren lands, and freezing nights seemed perpetual. At the earth's poles, vast quantities of snow fell at such a rate that it could not melt. Instead, it piled up to unprecedented heights. The pressure from the top was so immense that the snow at the bottom was turned into gigantic ice layers. These ice fields cooled the climates. The cycle intensified; more snow continued to fall, more ice continued to form, and the climate became colder. An oppressive frozen sheet, more than a mile thick, carved valleys and created mountains, as its fingers slowly grew and crept, crossing into yet unnamed continents.

And then, just as quickly, within a few thousand years, the natural balance of earth saw the glacial sheet retreat. As it moved back over the terrains it had scoured earlier, it reshaped the earth's surface anew. The planet had seen many ice ages in the past, and would see many more, before the evolution of humans and our current time.

Today, British Columbians live and travel in the beautiful valleys left behind by the sculpting forces of those frozen waters. The planet's chilly past is now long gone from a human perspective, but there are regions on the globe where ice age remnants still exist. Perhaps nowhere are these remnants more prevalent than in BC, where pockets of glacial ice linger, tucked deep within the mountain ranges of the province. Rugged, soaring in reach, a vivid sight to behold on any clear day, the countless peaks of BC are themselves a reminder of the planet's violent past.

There is one region, known to but a few, which sends a mountain lover's passion to new heights, the scenery more breathtaking than most. The Bugaboos, or 'Bugs', as seasoned rock climbers affectionately call them, are known for their distinctive spires, many of which soar to over 3000 metres, splendidly shaped by the erosive forces of ice and harsh mountain climates over the millennia.

When prospectors first penetrated these steep mountain valleys in the late 1800s they brought back word of the spectacular Spires to the outside world. The Bugaboos became a magnet for renowned mountaineers who began to visit the region as early as 1910.

The Bugaboo Spires are located in Bugaboo Provincial Park, nestled along the western edge of the Rocky Mountains. The Park is most often accessed from Parson or Brisco on Highway 95 out of Golden. However, instead of using these more traveled routes to view the Spires, we opted for a network of old and infrequently traveled backroads from the southwest. According to maps, this trail network in the Howser watershed does not penetrate the Park, but it does come within scratching distance.

The Howser Main FSR is a road for the well-prepared backroad explorer. The remoteness of this valley will appeal to anyone who likes winding shelf roads on cliffs, is comfortable with a multiple day walk to the nearest settlement, knows how to behave in grizzly bear country, and is equipped with a VHF radio to monitor logging traffic. An unexpected meeting with an oncoming logging truck on certain trail sections might cause considerable unease.

Our plans were to explore the Howser watershed to find a sub-alpine route that granted us a view of the magnificent Bugaboo Spires and the surrounding ice fields. We completed this trip in one long day.

Be aware... this is grizzly bear territory. Act accordingly.

On the Trail...

As we entered the Howser FSR, the trail sign indicated 'Active Hauling'. I entered the posted logging frequency into our VHF radio and broadcasted our position before proceeding. The route quickly gained elevation. The entrance to the Howser watershed became narrower, turning into a canyon with sheer walls out of which the tiny shelf road had been painstakingly blasted. The canyon then turned into a gorge, constricted by ever-higher walls of solid rock. Far below us the glacial waters of Howser Creek compressed to a frothing cauldron, sweeping at terrific speed over unseen rocks and boulders. Cautiously we followed the winding road. I silently commended the engineers and skilled workers who had carved this perilous route, and threw in a prayer for our own well-being. Above us lone dwarfed and twisted trees clung precariously to ledges, inexplicably sucking water out of solid rock. This stretch of road may not appeal to all, especially if you suffer from vertigo. It is often not wide enough for two vehicles to pass one another. Stay alert to the road conditions as your gaze may wander with the scenery; a second or two of inattention could result in a long fall from the narrow pass. There are no railings or side guards offering a second chance.

During this stretch I called out my position on the radio every few kilometres; luckily no one replied. Encountering another vehicle here, especially a loaded logging truck, would require quick thinking and immediate gear shifting. I made a mental note of the infrequent pullouts as I passed them, in case I encountered traffic further on and would have to back up to one of them.

As the Howser Creek canyon walls surrendered to a widening valley, we were granted a brief glimpse of the Four Squatters Glacier. This was the only viewing possibility of this gigantic glacier from the Howser Main.

We stopped to refill our canteens from a waterfall. Behind us a whitetail doe appeared, effortlessly cleared the gravel road bed with one jump, and stopped to watch us, her ears on high alert. The roar of the nearby runoff waters had likely muffled our passing. We waited as the deer slowly approached us; her curiosity driving her ever closer. Finally, she caught our scent and turned. Her long tail, brownish black on top and snowy white underneath, was raised like a flag as she leaped out of sight and down the embankment.

After a few more kilometres the road crossed back to the south side of the creek. Here it again climbed up sheer walls. As before, I called out our position on the radio every few minutes. While traveling up the Duncan FSR earlier that morning I had heard a logging truck driver announce his position on the Howser Main. Now all was quiet on the radio waves. I assumed that the driver was waiting for the truck to be loaded with logs and would announce his position once back in gear. This could be anywhere ahead of us.

As we bounced down the trail, we passed logged areas from previous years, breaking the contours of the forest. Still, many old-growth hemlocks, their massive trunks and arms providing shade and cool to the forest floor, lined the way. Somehow this easy bounty had so far escaped the chainsaws. A large pyramid-shaped mountain came into view: Virgin Mountain. Photo opportunities for this mountain improved with every turn of the road.

We passed Tea Creek FSR on our right near the 53km marker. My research indicated a large number of old mining claims were staked in that watershed. Unfortunately, counter to our original plans, our time schedule did not allow for exploring the area at that time. Instead my eyes scoured the mountain ridges that lined the sweeping valley as we pressed east. I was on the lookout for any sign of an old or new trail that might provide us access to the alpine and a view into Bugaboo Park. We took several promising side roads and cuts, all of which eventually dead-ended or were too overgrown to pass. We were constantly backtracking to the Main. After several hours, our disappointment growing, we felt tired and hungry. If there truly was an access route to the alpine on this side of the park we had not discovered it.

Then our radio speaker crackled. The logging truck driver that I heard earlier that morning gave his position as not too far ahead of us and we replied with our position. He answered, indicating that he would wait for us at the Teneese Creek Bridge to allow us to pass by one another.

Approaching Virgin Mountain

During our trailside conversation with the driver he confirmed that, indeed, views into the Bugaboos were possible from the area and gave us directions. After parting ways we crossed Teneese Creek. Our spirits renewed, and immensely thankful

69

for our sudden good fortune, we proceeded up Rory FSR, past Leaning Rock and then up Spur 100.

The trail here was even narrower and several times steeper than the canyon section we had traversed earlier. As the number of mountain roads that I explore increases, so does my respect and admiration for the courageous men and women who navi-

On backroads, always watch for loaded logging trucks

gate these tiny ledges with loaded logging trucks weighing tens of thousands of pounds; one moment of inattention and their fate is sealed. Runaway lanes are a luxury found only on modern highways. Here your life depends upon your alertness and the mechanical soundness of your rig.

Up, up, up our little engine pulled us into the wide-open sky. All around us mountain peaks and snowfields slowly emerged. The tight switchbacks continued ever higher. At approximately the 61km marker there was a brief glimpse of the

Spires just through the forest tips: a harbinger of the view to come. At a Y in the road we stayed left. The deactivations now became numerous and deep; slowly, careful not to bottom out

Leaning Rock near Rory Creek

the springs, I feathered the throttle to bring the rear through to the far crest. Over and over, we continuously climbed in and out of the cross ditches. I lost count after one hundred. To our left tremendous views of the pale blue Four Squatters Glacier emerged, oozing like frozen lava onto the rocky alpine ridges beneath it. It looked the size of a small city. Just when I thought we had chosen the wrong trail out popped the 'Bugs', within a hundred feet of the trail's end.

We stopped and climbed out of the truck. The mountain air was crisp and cool. Some people are most at home along the oceans, others are in love with the grasslands of the prairies. For me there is no place as inspiring as being among remote mountain peaks. We stood in the middle of that great amphitheatre headlining the Spires; the scenery was incredible. The lead role was unequivocally granted to the Howser Spire: at

Howser Peak

almost 3400 metres it was a mammoth. There were no ridges, there were no vistas, just endless cliff faces, too steep for even snow to accumulate. In supporting roles, to the right, almost one half a kilometre less in height, but no less enrapturing, was Howser Peak, and tucked in between the two behemoths was the Bugaboo Glacier, barely visible above the tree tips at the trail's end. Over millions of years, erosive mountain weather and glacial ice forces have ground the granite into the shapes we admired that day. As we stood and watched, I felt anew what a little figure humankind presents in our great wilderness and how short our stay on this planet has been so far.

Tailgate lunch at 1,860 metres

With our altimeter pegged at 1860 metres, Karen prepared a scrumptious tailgate lunch while Keera helped me sniff out optimal photo locations.

Despite a two-hour long visit on our private lookout, the cloud cover never completely disappeared from the Spires. Like a beautiful woman draped behind a white veil, the Bugs remained reluctant to reveal their full magnificence. After lunch we explored through the alpine meadows. Daisies and paint brushes were everywhere; we collected a bag of mountain arnica for tea. Finally, time obliged us to return to the valleys.

Riel Marquardt

Collecting mountain arnica,
the Four Squatters in the background

We continued north along Rory Creek, past a helicopter refueling station for the winter heli-ski season and over the bridge to the north side of the creek. Roads here had not been traveled in years. As we tried to push further they eventually became so overgrown that I could no longer walk along them, much less drive. We retraced our steps to the Teneese Creek Bridge and pointed our truck eastward into the Teneese watershed. My hope was to find another alpine vista road for more 'Bugs' photos. After several kilometres we took a turn south into an unnamed watershed. Large stands of old growth hemlock again guarded the way. I attempted to penetrate several old cut-block roads but the brush growth was just too dense. Nature had now reclaimed these roads from man. Eventually we turned around, back to the Teneese Creek Main and followed it east until we came to an old wooden bridge.

Unsure as to its condition I checked it on foot. I saw steel girders under the aged wood planking and we drove on. At certain sections, where the trail side undergrowth was not too dense, we inched past magnificent old growth cedars.

Grown-in trail along Teneese Creek

The trail paralleled Teneese Creek for several kilometres. We again crossed countless cross ditches. Perhaps the equipment operator responsible for digging the deactivations in these mountains had been paid piecemeal and not by the hour, I joked to Karen as we jostled through another cross ditch. She was too busy hanging on to reply.

Finally we reached a switchback, the first sign of access to the alpine. It was now 5:00 pm and we sat and deliberated. From here we would require at least three hours back to our camp on Duncan Lake. Heading uphill now might or might not give us access to the alpine region in this valley. We felt it prudent to turn around. Up and down through all the deactivations we returned: windows up as we passed through heavily brushed sections of the trail, quickly down again to cool our cab in the hot afternoon temperatures. Despite our best efforts our cab was soon filled with trail side inhabitants: spiders, flies, caterpillars and other unknown insects of all colours were scraped off their leafy homes and deposited into our laps. On one section we baked in the heat for what seemed like forever. We were forced to keep our windows up as a deer-fly attacked our truck. It was absolutely determined to enter our cab. We had to protect ourselves against this tiny insect's angry persistence. Admittedly, air conditioning does have its merits.

Up and down went the windows again until the trail widened. As the deactivations ceased we rounded a corner close to the rushing creek. And there it stood. Tall, big...simply majestic, no other word was fitting. A grizzly, with chocolate brown fur, stood on its hind legs. Like a dancing acrobat, its massive claws gently pawed the air to help keep its balance. The animal occupied the trail perhaps twenty feet ahead of us, its massive body at a right angle to our travel direction. Its round head and snout lifted high into the air, moving in small semicircles, sniffing intently. Perhaps it had been dining on tender grass shoots along the creek, sensed our presence and, now curious, climbed up the short embankment for a better look. We were uninvited intruders into its home and it had to determine our whereabouts. Not daring to speak, Karen and I sat still in the idling truck, the creek drowning out the engine sounds. Keera was deep asleep in the truck bed and did not stir. Fresh bear scat had decorated the trail for sometime now and this was obviously the perpetrator.

Trailside life comes in all shapes and sizes

The king of the forest took a staggered step backward, shifting its position. It now faced us square on. Its deep black muzzle, centered in its dishpan face, continued to test the warm afternoon air, determined to pluck any scents out of the ordinary. The bear had a huge frame, which to my layman eyes appeared well over seven feet tall. I suddenly felt small and insignificant, even inside our truck. The bear's shaggy appearance was that of an unkempt and tattered mountain dweller, its fur-coat hanging as if several sizes too large - a sign of molting season. The bear looked un-fearful, almost docile, while balancing in front of us. In slow motion I leaned out the open window with my camera...this would make a prize-winning photo. The instant I penetrated the air space outside the truck cab the grizzly must have caught my scent. In a blink the animal dropped on all fours, turned its bulk with amazing agility and broke into a gallop down the middle of the trail away from us. Its large back muscles tightened and released with every bounce, hiding the bear's head from our sight. It gathered immense speed with every foot of ground it put between us. The animal vanished around a bend a hundred feet away, a small dust cloud left behind.

Spectacular! I had read that grizzly bears were extremely fast and that a human being had no chance of outrunning one. The latter statement had always been difficult for me to believe. After all, I reasoned, how fast could an animal that weighed 400 to 500 pounds possibly be? I had naively convinced myself that, if ever confronted, I would try to outrun a bear, not because of my past achievements in track and field, but simply because I seriously doubted the fact that a large bear could out-sprint me. Now that I had witnessed its agility and speed I was convinced: no human could match that pace. With reverence and anticipation we slowly drove down the trail, not wanting to alarm the bear further, all the while hoping for another sighting. But the bear was gone for good. Its paw marks veered off the trail just after the bend, uphill, through a seemingly impenetrable tangle of fallen logs. From the safety of our truck I studied the grizzly's prints. Unlike a black bear, which has its claw indentations just ahead of the toe marks, the grizzly leaves claw marks several inches in front of its feet, due to the longer curved design of its claws. This particular grizzly had its claw marks two to three inches ahead of its toes, indicating its formidable size.

We rambled down the trail again, surprised at our repeated good fortune, sighting within the same day the Bugaboo Spires and a grizzly bear. Both were the biggest specimens in their own realm and yet, despite their enormous sizes, difficult to locate and view.

It was a long, dusty drive back down the Howser Main. We saw no further wildlife - although with our discussion of grizzly bears, perhaps we just did not notice any. During more than twelve hours of backroad exploring that day we encountered one vehicle, the logging truck near the Teneese Bridge.

In Reflection...

To travel down the Howser Main and explore its side-shoots is a trip into the superlatives. Far from the nearest settlement, its vast stretches of tiny roads, many now reclaimed by Nature, are braved only by the occasional logging truck driver. Ancient glaciers and granite peaks that few British Columbians have ever heard of, and fewer yet will ever see, are hidden within its deepest reaches.

This is the home of the largest of all land carnivores, the massive grizzly bear. This is a place to ponder the mystery of Nature, to touch an old hemlock tree that was alive before Columbus arrived on this continent. And, if you look closely at that very tree, perhaps it will be marked with claws, a natural signpost along a well-worn and traveled path of a particular grizzly.

It is a long drive into the Howser watershed to enjoy a peek in the Bugaboos, and it is worth it.

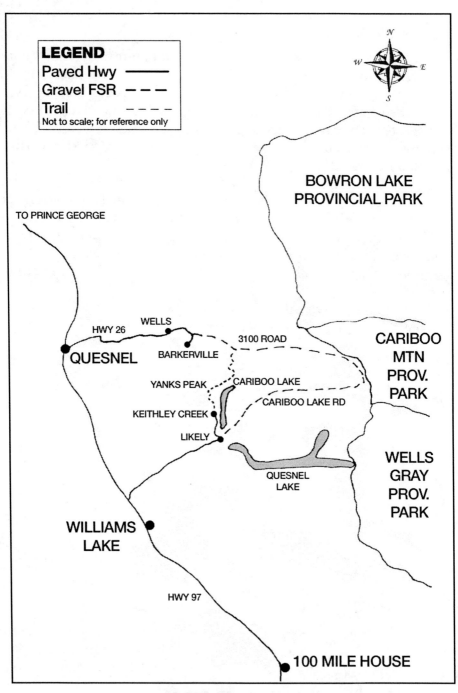

BARKERVILLE LOOP

Barkerville Sunshine

'And where you trod muddy roads and precipitous trails, a mighty highway now bears its traffic of giant transport trucks, fast cars, mobile homes and modern coaches, covering your laborious journey of five weeks in a matter of hours.'

In the Beginning...

The preceding quote is from *The Cariboo Dream*, a book published in 1971 by F.W. Lindsay. The 'muddy roads and precipitous trails' refer to the original Cariboo Gold Rush Trail and the 'mighty highway' is Highway 97, the modern blacktop ribbon which now closely follows the old trail. As a young man in the early 1900s Lindsay worked in Barkerville, BC, a small mining town born in the heart of the 1860s Cariboo Gold Rush country. Some of the old prospectors and pioneers from the gold rush days shared their stories and life memories with him.

Lindsay's book chronicles the journey of 26 Welshmen, as told through the pages of two diaries kept by a pair of the gold-seekers. In 1862 these hardy adventurers left their families in Wales, Great Britain, and for the next six months travelled by sailing ship half way around the globe. They arrived in New Westminster, BC, the one-time capital of the province. They spent the next five weeks struggling on foot across the 500 miles of hastily built and primitive Cariboo Gold Rush Trail, to finally arrive in the Barkerville area. That is when the real work began!

They staked claims on Lightning Creek and mined tirelessly for the next several years. The two diaries share just how extreme the conditions were for these Welsh miners. Their trip was financed with limited capital and they were supplied with tools which were useless for placer mining. It was a gamble against time, mud, water, inexperience, sickness, personal animosities and even mutiny. They did it in the hopes of finding the precious metal being uncovered in vast quantities around them.

The Cariboo Gold Rush has the distinction of being one of the richest placer gold rushes in world history. Though the exact figure of gold extracted will never be known, it is estimated to be in the hundreds of millions of dollars. During its peak, some mines reportedly drew in excess of $10,000 a day in gold.

Following historic footsteps

Needless to say, depending on Lady Luck, the Welsh miners' combined efforts had the potential to make them extremely wealthy.

Our own trip to explore the historic Cariboo area would take us along portions of the old Cariboo Gold Rush Trail, past famous gold creeks, including Lightning Creek, into Barkerville and beyond. Unlike the miners in Lindsay's book who took weeks, we could comfortably travel in a matter of hours the old route to the Cariboo, now called Highway 97.

Gold Rush Trail now silent and waiting...

On the Trail...

It was early morning when we met our camping companions, Kari and Lucy, in the town of Clinton. Originally known as 47 Mile House it was given its present name in 1863 in honour of Henry Pelham Clinton, the 5th Duke of Newcastle. I wondered if the good Duke had ever even set foot in this dusty road stop.

It was a warm sunny day and we assumed it was the start

to beautiful weather for our entire trip. Our two vehicles, fully loaded with a week's worth of camping supplies, headed north on the highway. The original Cariboo Road was visible in places often only a short distance from the pavement's edge: a thin grassy line, sometimes above the highway, sometimes below, at other times overgrown and forgotten, hidden under towering trees and guarded by farmers' barbwire.

We passed through other original gold trail stops: 100 Mile House, 108 Mile House and 150 Mile House. These names originated with the building of the Gold Rush Trail. The road houses were simply called by the mileage marker locations on the trail as measured from Lillooet, the starting point of the trek to the Barkerville gold fields. The road houses offered food and shelter for the travelling prospectors and were usually a day's walk apart. The heritage site at 108 Mile House still has numerous original buildings and can be toured from May to October. A visit is an enjoyable step back in time.

North to Quesnel we continued. Quesnel was named after Jules Maurice Quesnel. He was a member of Simon Fraser's historic exploration party that descended the Fraser Canyon by canoe in 1808, the first known Europeans to have done so.

As we drove over the blacktop I let my eyes wander onto another section of the old trail. This was where the thousands of prospectors had actually set foot en-route to their dreams of unlimited wealth. The first ones to enter this country came in small parties, three or four men to a group. They sampled every creek. If the gravel paid, a little town sprang up overnight. It vanished just as quickly when new discoveries were made further upstream. Every strike, every creek, became a stepping stone to the El Dorado that every miner was convinced existed. Drawn by this invisible force, these early prospectors methodically pushed ever deeper and further into the unexplored hills, like bloodhounds on a scent, able to endure any hardship until the yellow prey was cornered.

After these first scouts brought back word of the riches to be had, countless more followed. They came from all over the world, separately and in large groups, each one sure the big find would happen that day or maybe tomorrow, or the next day.

I imagined the group of 26 Welshmen lumbering along the nearby trail; they carried packs and gear while guiding their heavily laden horses. Each member was filled with his own dreams of striking it rich in the wilderness, and perhaps already planning how to spend their fortunes. I wondered if they were boisterous and loud, looking forward to their new home or quiet and demure, in awe of their surroundings and fully aware of their upcoming challenges.

Quesnel, the Gold Pan City

Karen suddenly interrupted my day dreaming to point out that I should turn on the windshield wipers. Hopefully just a shower I remarked, as we would be wilderness tenting for the remainder of our trip. I set the wipers to intermittent.

A few hours later in Quesnel I was obliged to set the wipers to continuous. We reassured one another the rain would soon stop.

We turned onto Highway 26, the Barkerville Highway, and headed east into the hills. At a spot on Lightning Creek we halted for the day. Moods were dampened, but not extinguished by the rains as we set up our tents. It took a while to get the fire crackling, but we eventually succeeded and retired early that night to the coziness of our sleeping bags.

The next morning the weather consisted of heavy rain with periods of heavier rain. The inside of our tent hung heavy with water pellets from the humidity. Undaunted, we spent the

Panning on Lightning Creek

morning exploring Lightning Creek. Everywhere were signs of old mining operations. We dipped our gold pans into the famous waters. With every pan I eagerly awaited gold specs to emerge as the gravel and sand slowly washed away. Pan after pan, spot after spot we tried, but eventually we returned to our campsite empty handed. Again my imagination floated back to the 26 Welshmen who staked their claims on this creek. I wondered how long they toiled before they struck it rich.

We gave up waiting for the sun to appear and after lunch we packed our wet gear and headed east towards Wells. This little town was born during the Great Depression. Fred Wells, the founder of the town in 1932, started the Cariboo Gold Quartz Mine. By the time the gold reserves dwindled in 1966 it had produced over $25 million in gold. We stopped in the restored Wells Hotel, which was built in 1933. Inside we enjoyed a drink in the historical atmosphere and, to everybody's delight, soaked up the warmth and dryness. After a lengthy visit, our clothes now dry, we climbed back into our trucks and made for our next campsite for the night. We fully anticipated better weather tomorrow.

On the 3100 Road we turned off at the Whiskey Flats Recreation Site near the historically significant Antler Creek. It was in this creek that the first gold discovery in the region was made by four prospectors in 1860 which, in turn, sparked the greatest gold rush in the history of Canada. Our plans were to camp here for the next five days and explore the area in depth.

We were in bed by dusk, despite having to crawl into wet tents and damp sleeping bags.

Morning dawned with the same weather as the night before. No matter, we were exploring and after breakfast we drove into Barkerville for the day.

Of all the ghost towns in BC, Barkerville is surely the best known. Perhaps it can be argued that it is not a ghost town at all. Rather, it is a living museum with its ghosts very much alive: actors dressed in period clothing inhabit the town during tourist season. During the gold rush days it was called the largest community west of Chicago and north of San Francisco. Most of the buildings in Barkerville were elevated, since with the surrounding hillsides stripped of every single tree to line mine shafts or construct buildings, the valley bottom received the resultant water runoff and liquid earth. Environmentalists must have been busy panning as well. The buildings, erected in the Williams Creek Valley, consisted of banks, restaurants, churches, butcher shops, hotels and more.

The town now looks much as it did in the late 1800s, with a

main street and miners' cabins scattered chaotically among vacant lots. Saloon-keepers, grocers, barbers, gamblers, dancing girls, photographers, newspapermen all nodded knowingly to each other across the muddy main street of this bonanza town.

Barkerville, a ghost town very much alive

Tens of thousands of fortune seekers braved the Cariboo trails with Barkerville as their destination at some point in their travels.

One of those fortune seekers was the infamous William 'Billy'

Barker, after whom Barkerville was named. He deserted his whaling ship in Victoria and joined the exodus to the Cariboo. His claim on Williams Creek hit a rich lode at the bottom of a 52-foot-deep shaft. Records state that Billy and his partners hauled up over $600,000 in gold from their hole: a fantastic sum of money for that time period, the equivalent of $30 million today. Amazingly, Barker was broke and living in the Old Man's Home in Victoria when he died 30 years later.

Today Barkerville has over 130 restored buildings looking much like it did in the late 1800s. The town transcends time.

Despite the rainy weather the streets were busy with tourists being entertained by the talented and good humoured street actors. During one tour we caught our first glimpse of Barkerville bullion. One of the actors pulled out a considerable sized nugget from his chest pocket, and with an attentive eye passed it among the spectators. It was amazingly heavy for such a small object.

As the crowds started to thin late in the day, Karen and I tried our hand at panning at a tourist sluice next to the gift shop. Under the guidance of the attendant, who had just returned victoriously from the World Gold Panning Championships, we finally hit pay dirt! Well ok, a few gold flakes from a spiked pan. None-the-less, we finally had some authentic Cariboo gold to lay claim to. Best of all, the recently crowned champion gave us pointers in the gold panning department that would hopefully improve our chances of finding some gold on our own.

With a lull in the rain we headed back to our campsite. That evening around another struggling fire we glimpsed the stars for a while. It gave us hope for a weather improvement. We crawled into damp sleeping bags inside even damper tents that night. The next morning the skies were still pastel grey, the rains intermittent. We decided to explore the historic mountain pass over Yank's Peak. As mentioned, the first big strike in the Cariboo was made by a group of four seasoned prospectors: Doc Keithley, George Weaver, Benjamin McDonald and John Rose. In the fall of 1860 they set out for new diggings in the uncharted Cariboo Mountains. They came upon the as yet unnamed Antler Creek and proceeded to pan the richest deposits discovered in the province to that date. As they stared at their pans full of nuggets, instead of the usual flakes prospectors were finding along the Fraser River, their instincts kicked in. They swore one another to secrecy. When they returned to the Keithley Creek General Store the next day for supplies, either through an incautious word or action, the word got out. Their find started the ensuing gold stampede to the Cariboo treasure chest, the land of Golden Promise, and further discoveries of even richer gold deposits along numerous other creeks. In the years to follow, gold would be removed by the ton.

The Yank's Peak four-wheel drive trail follows, in part, the original route into this wild country taken by the four veteran gold seekers and all that initially followed. The route served for many years as a packing trail for prospectors in and out of the area. It was later replaced by a wagon trail to the west.

We arrived at the turnoff to Yanks Peak marked by a large sign indicating summer travel by four-wheel drive only. If you do visit this historically significant trail a few rules of common courtesy and good sense are in order. Please leave buildings and mining relics the way you found them. Travel on well established trails only; do not take, or create, any unauthorized shortcuts. There is talk of a Motorized Recreation Regulation Order being put into effect as mindless characters have been tearing up the alpine meadows causing damage. Actions of a careless few may shut down the trail for everybody. Lock your hubs at the bottom and activate low gear before continuing on. Ensure your passengers and gear are secured. For most backroad explorers this is a challenging and enjoyable drive. Extra lift and bigger tires will be of benefit. If you feel intimidated early on in the trip, turn around. The trail does not improve with elevation. As with many BC mountain trails the overgrowth increases with altitude and the trail becomes more aggressive.

With Kari and Lucy in the lead we headed up. We navigated across countless ruts, ledges, and steep off-camber

Panning on Yank's Peak

sections with loose rock. Hairpins connected muddy washouts. We stuck to the main trail.

Our tummies signaled a lunch stop next to a crumbling mine entrance; deep inside the shaft jagged rafters cut the black ness. At a nearby creek, and with yesterday's panning lessons still fresh, we dipped our pans anew. After each fruitless pan full we found ourselves moving further up the creek, excited and convinced that an overlooked nugget must lie beneath the next tree root or around the next creek bend. Perhaps the tumbling waters and surrounding trees recognized our kind from over the decades: ghost-coloured people brandishing over-size saucers, shaking sand and gravel to and fro inside of them as if possessed - wondering when we would finally leave again. We gave it our best shot but after several hours we found ourselves back in our trucks, our clothes full of rain, and our pans empty. Either our panning skills were still lacking or we were simply a century too late. I am sure the creek and trees smiled knowingly as we left them in peace again.

With Kari and Lucy still in the lead we forged further up the pass. As Kari navigated a particularly tight hairpin, we heard a loud crack followed by the unmistakeable sound of escaping air. We got out, already aware of what we might see. Sure enough, the 4Runner sat cockeyed, leaning heavily to the passenger side. The right rear mud tire was flat as a door mat, not a pound of air left inside. The smoking gun, a thick snag, was still protruding out of the side wall; it had ripped a large hole into the black rubber. Kari made a remark about needing a 'tree terrain' tire, not a mud terrain tire. Quite a calm response considering he had just ruined a $200-plus tire. Out came all the camping gear from the back of his truck to get at the buried high-lift jack. While the drizzle continued, Kari and I replaced the ruined tire with the spare.

Soon we were rolling again, our eyes alert as ever to trail side debris. As we left the switchbacks behind us, and the ground leveled, we were met by a stiff breeze. Around us fog banks swirled; the rains, sometimes intermixed with hail now, fell in heavy bursts. The wind rocked our trucks as we approached the peak. One final narrow hill climb and we were at the top, well above the 6000-foot mark where the snows lingered until July and returned by September. We realized the fog banks were actually passing clouds, being forced about by high elevation winds like sheep by a dog. We sat in our respective trucks, communicated by CB and watched Nature's drama unfold around us. No one volunteered to step outside. At times the storm clouds parted briefly, and gave us impressive views of the distant Wells Gray Provincial Park. It was now late afternoon and we pointed our steeds back down the mountain.

Back at our Antler Creek campsite that night, we gave up on starting a campfire in the rain for a third time. We also agreed to move on the next morning, hoping for some improvement in weather once further east. Karen and Lucy complained of cold symptoms as we climbed into our wet tents and sleeping gear for the third straight night. We all tried to make the best of our situation. As I lay awake that night, my thoughts drifted between my nice dry bed at home and my current sleeping arrangements. I pondered how the prospectors of over a century and a half ago coped with prolonged rains. They spent months or even years here. We had had enough after three days. When ill weather engulfed the roaming adventurers they

Heading east toward Wells Grey Park

had to stick it out in canvas tents, if they were lucky. They were more likely in tree-covered holes in the ground. Unlike our current time, they had no vehicles to warm up in, or enable them a quick escape to a drier climate. No wonder the average age on the headstones we had seen near Barkerville was well below forty. One simply had to marvel at the toughness of the Cariboo pioneers.

The next morning the skies were still grey but the rains had finally stopped. Spirits ran higher. We hit the 3100 Road eastward. The 3100 Road is a modern and wide logging road, wide enough for a herd of elephants when compared to yesterday's crawl up Yank's Peak. And then... Eureka! For the first time in days sunshine reflected off our hood as we approached the Wells Grey Park boundary. Our spirits were now as high as the sun as we neared the snow dusted mountains to the east. Like the prospectors of yesteryear we had endured and finally came out victorious. We stopped at Ghost Lake for lunch. I whipped out my gold pan hoping to rescue a few specks from a stream. No luck. I consoled myself by surmising that we were too far from Barkerville.

After lunch we followed the Cariboo Lake Logging Road until we reached a beautiful camp site on Cariboo Lake; the recent rains had ensured complete vacancy for us. Under blue skies I tried my hand at more gold panning. I came up with two tiny flakes. Yes! This was surely a sign that our fortune had changed. Before dinner we bathed in the lake and then soaked up the sun's heavenly warmth. Our campsite resembled an Asian bazaar, multi-coloured clothes and gear hung everywhere, as we tapped Nature's drying power.

That night our laughter echoed far across the waters. For the first time on the trip we sat up late around the campfire enjoying not being wet and connecting with the star studded night. We congratulated ourselves for having 'stuck it out'. We had outlasted the ill weather.

The next morning I opened the tent flap and expected to be blinded by golden rays. I received a face full of water: courtesy of the tent fly. It was raining again, and just as hard as the previous days. The sun was gone and the sky had returned to grey on grey. Kari emerged from his tent-trailer and we threw each other disgruntled glances. Slowly we went about our breakfast preparations. Karen and Lucy had their colds back. We agreed to cut our Cariboo trip short and head towards a lake near Clinton. We quietly packed away everything in our trucks and headed south.

Near the hamlet of Likely we stopped at a creek canyon which had been hydrauliced over a century ago. It might as well have happened yesterday, as the canyon walls were completely barren with no vegetation finding a foothold on the exposed bedrock. Hydraulicing is the use of high pressured water cannons to wash all the topsoil off a gold-bearing hillside. The silt and gravel are flushed through sluices, where it is separated and the gold recovered. The resulting total lack of topsoil on the earth's surface obliterates the chance of any plant life from growing in the area for years, if ever. The evidence of the ruined landscape lay in front of us, stark and still.

We emerged back onto Highway 97 and continued south. In Clinton, with the relentless rains still falling, we agreed to call it quits and parted on our respective ways for home.

On our trip to the Cariboo Gold Country, the gleam of Barkerville sunshine seemed as difficult to locate as Barkerville gold.

In Reflection...

You may wonder what happened to the intrepid 26 Welshmen chronicled in Lindsay's book. The men worked like slaves on numerous shafts for two years on Lightening Creek. They faced insurmountable odds and in the end gained nothing but experience. Despite their brawn and courage and the fortunes being unearthed from the gravel around them by others, the Welsh miners returned to Wales just as penniless as they had departed years earlier. Their leader, John Evans, one of the diary authors, remained in the Cariboo. He never did strike it rich in the gold fields. However, he was elected as the Cariboo Representative to the Provincial Parliament in 1875. Here, he served the Cariboo people until his death in 1879. He is buried near Barkerville.

In the Cariboo the ghosts from the centuries before still cling to towns long dead, abandoned cabins and crumbling mines – determined trailbreakers and prospectors, saloon-keepers and dance girls, gamblers and men of God. These were the everyday people who rose to extraordinary challenges in this extraordinary land, the Cariboo of BC. Everyone dreamed of taking the yellow dust home, to find a quick fortune. Many did... but many more did not.

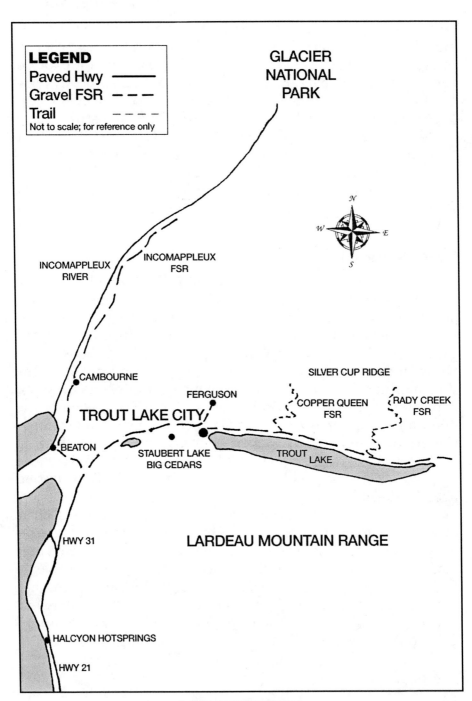

LARDEAU TRAILS

Legends of the Lardeau

...we suddenly felt alone and vulnerable in this part of the high country, thankful to have at least some protection from the violent storm.

In the Beginning...

We set up camp early on Arrow Lake. After dinner, we relaxed in front of our little campfire, darkness slowly descending upon the tree-lined beachhead. At our feet the lake shimmered in the light of a full moon. Far to the south of us, we watched a distant Kootenay thunderstorm. An impenetrable wall of blackness, it crept across the open waters and then slowly and deliberately engulfed the Valhalla Mountains one peak at a time. Bolts of lightning illuminated the night sky every few seconds, then not at all, filling our heightened senses with anticipation. Our eyes glued to the skyline, we did not want to look away for fear of missing another scene in one of Nature's most graphic displays of energy. Keera, our dog, moved restlessly between our chairs, groaning and repositioning herself with every thunder boom that echoed throughout the steep valleys across the lake from us. Her sensitive ears always made her uncomfortable around thunder. Karen and I did not talk. We did not want to interrupt the powerful spell the storm had cast upon us. We had long ago lost track of time and accepted the arrival of windblown raindrops from the distant storm as a signal that all shows must come to an end. Reluctantly, we left our ringside seats and sought refuge in our small tent for the night. Still entranced by Nature's energy we fell asleep while the Kootenay water drops gently kissed our shelter goodnight.

Riel Marquardt

The next morning when I awoke I was aware of a presence before even opening my eyes. I kept them closed, focusing on my sense of hearing. There it was again, much closer this time; a soft rap, quick and successive. Then again, right above us

Eagles' mating dance

this time. Karen, who was also listening, was unable to contain her curiosity and crawled out of the tent. The shrill cry of an eagle greeted her as she stood up outside. I opened my eyes and was out of the tent in an instant. We observed a Bald Eagle, stately perched in a nearby tree, perhaps fifty feet above us. It had picked the very top of the tallest tree, its dark plumage boldly outlined against the blue summer sky. With its snow-white head slightly cocked in our direction it let out another piercing call, as if scolding us for sleeping in. Then, somewhat indignant, it turned its head away and ignored us, confident that even at this close range we could do it no harm.

Karen and I pulled up our camping chairs. We moved slowly to prevent alarming the large bird of prey. Trading the binoculars back and forth, we enthusiastically examined our magnificent morning friend. The raptor apparently enjoyed our attention as it started to preen and clean itself with meticulous detail, at peace with itself and its surroundings.

To Native North Americans the eagle represents heroic nobility and the Great Spirit. These birds were seen as messengers from heaven and embodied the spirit of the sun. The Natives considered the feathers of eagles to be sacred and they are still used in traditional healing ceremonies today. Suddenly our personal Nature feature was kicked into high gear. Without warning, like a stone out the sky, a second eagle appeared into our field of vision, plummeting straight down out of the heavens. It continued to free fall, its feathered body creating an unbelievably loud hissing noise as it sliced the crisp air, plunging ever faster towards the perched eagle. A split second before the plunging eagle reached it, the perched eagle gently lifted off. It rolled sideways and the two raptors locked talons directly above our heads. Like two medieval combatants, the pair of eagles appeared locked in a death struggle. They rolled and fell; their bodies a blur of white and brown, still linked together. They accelerated as they somersaulted through free space again and again. Avoiding a collision with Mother Earth by a mere split second, they separated on cue several feet above us. The air movement of their six-foot wingspans brushed our faces as they strafed our tent site and headed out over the lake where they parted ways. This mystical form of sky dancing we had been privileged to witness is part of the eagles' mating ritual. It reflected the excitement and joy of the sexual energy these fierce and independent Bald Eagles shared with one another. Our mouths were open in awe: what an honour. Grateful, we looked at one another. We both agreed... there could be no better start to our trip to the legendary Lardeau.

On the Trail...

The instant I saw the picture I knew I had to explore the area. My backroad explorer's heart beat faster just looking at it. A road – no, a goat trail made slightly wider by balancing rocks and laying split timbers on any support that could be found – was pinned to the rock walled canyon. Below raged the

The Incommapleux Bridge of yesterday

Incomappleux River, known to locals as the Fish River. The trail was built in the late 1800s to connect the towns of Beaton and Camborne in the mineral rich Lardeau Country. And thus, from this picture my interest in this back and beyond area was born.

The Lardeau region lies hidden between towering mountain ranges in the Kootenays, the snow peaks and glaciers daring from afar the lonesome traveler to come discover the secrets of this area. Remote from major travel routes there are no 'passer-bys'; one has to plan to visit here. Most of the towns once built by confident mining prospectors are now reclaimed by the lush forests and vegetation. Fir, cedar, hemlock, cow parsnip and devils club thrive in this steep country watered by icy streams. They overgrow roads, bury rusted mining equipment and cover foundations of ruined buildings from long ago. Camborne, Beaton and Trout Lake City are chapters in the Lardeau history book that few remember today, yet they were once home to many. In order to enjoy this wild landscape one requires a keen sense of adventure. For the more intrepid backroad traveler there are still many passable routes leading to the ghosts of the area, hidden in deep valleys or on high alpine ridges.

Following our morning eagle visitation, we finished breakfast, and headed for the Needles ferry. The open-deck ferry crosses Arrow Lake by means of a large cable-pulley. The vessel crosses from Needles to Fauquier. A ferry has been in operation here since 1913. However, back then the two settlements were in two different locations. Fauquier was relocated to its present location and Needles disappeared when large parts of the Arrow Lakes were flooded in the 1960s with the construction of the Hugh Keenleyside Dam at Castlegar. The dam created a lake some 250 kilometres long and destroyed farms, summer homes and entire communities along the lakeshore.

We passed through the town of Nakusp, which with 1800 inhabitants is the largest town on the Upper Arrow Lake. North on Highway 23 we continued. Our goal was to locate the pass through the Incomappleux River canyon and continue to the ghost town of Camborne. It was built on the fortunes of the mines that were operated in the late 1800s to mid 1900s. Its fate was sealed in 1952 when, after a number of fires, the Sunshine Lardeau Mine completely suspended operations and Camborne eventually joined the ranks of the other ghost towns

101

in the Lardeau area.

We turned onto Highway 31, a wide gravel logging road. After a number of wrong turns and stops for route taking, I eventually located the Incomappleux trailhead. It was now an old logging road. As the valley started to close in on us, we realized the Incomappleux canyon must be near.

The Incomappleux River is born among the mammoth 10,000-foot plus mountains in Glacier National Park. It carves its passage through extremely remote and rough terrain, draining into the Upper Arrow Lake through the very canyon we were searching for. This narrow canyon also provides the only access road into the entire watershed. To my excitement, when we reached the canyon entrance the access road looked only slightly wider than in the century old picture that had initiated our visit. The swollen Incomappleux River frothing on the right, and the boulder strewn path, half carved from the granite canyon wall and half supported by a bridge type structure on the left were exactly as I had envisioned it would look. I was ecstatic. I asked Karen to take a picture while I drove across. Usually not keen on taking pictures, she readily agreed and hastily picked her way through the rocks and boulders to the other side. At that point I realized that she would rather walk than drive across the narrows.

Convinced that the 'half bridge' was perfectly stable I started across. Right at that point a pumpkin-size rock decided it had resisted gravity long enough. It let itself free from up above and landed in a puff of dust several car lengths in front of my hood. The roar of the river was deafening, drowning out any accompanying sound. I held my breath, steering around numerous boulders of all sizes that lay on the road, the most recent addition of which was already lost in the debris field. I continued on. I had waited a long time to explore this section of trail, but that experience left me unnerved. The potential for further rock fall and even slides was evident, and if a larger slide did occur in the canyon after we passed we would be stuck on the wrong side of the only access road into the watershed. I had seen no indication of active logging; this route could be closed indefinitely. I kept these thoughts to myself, not wanting to alarm Karen. Fortunately, no further gifts fell out of the sky and I reached the other side unscathed. We drove on for several kilometres, the road meandering along side the aqua-green river, its colours revealing its glacial origins. We stopped at an

The Incommapleux Bridge of today

old cabin, which required a closer inspection by Karen. As Keera pursued musty scents from long ago, Karen sleuthed for clues of the last inhabitants. Curiosities satisfied, we continued up the broad valley, leaving the Incomappleux River behind as we followed the trail into the forest. I had to lock the hubs to keep going up the road. It had now deteriorated into a muddy quagmire. My All-Terrain tires were definitely out-matched. The soupy mud laughed at our little four-wheel drive seeking passage. I struggled to maintain traction on numerous hills. I had to walk the tires from side to side, maintaining just the proper amount of throttle to ensure my forward momentum while seeking to prevent tire spin and the resulting loss of traction and control. On one particular hill, we slid back down, and after several attempts I thought winching would be the only recourse. I decided to give it one final try. I backed up an extra long way and pressed hard on the accelerator. Up we bounced, mud flying, engine screaming. Up, up, up and over – woohoo! Even Keera howled enthusiastically from the back of the truck as we crested the rise.

By mid afternoon, with no sign of the former Camborne townsite, we stopped for a tailgate lunch. I though about the pumpkin-size rocks falling in greater numbers in the river canyon and suggested we turn around and make for Trout Lake City.

With liberal use of the accelerator, and thankful to not get stuck, we traced our way back to gravel on Highway 31 and followed it east. Along Armstrong Lake, dining knee deep in the weeds, a cow moose and her offspring came into view. Above them two Bald Eagles circled, as if keeping guard on the valley's inhabitants. The moose watched our truck slowly approach, then turned and quietly disappeared into the brush as we stopped. The eagles also vanished. We drove on.

Trout Lake City lies on the northwest corner of Trout Lake. The 'city' grew very quickly in the 1890s, stimulated by the surrounding rich mines. At its peak the community had five hotels, a water system, a Canadian Imperial Bank of Commerce branch, a telephone network, a hospital, two general stores, a stage line linking it to communities in the west, and a steamship linking it to the Canadian Pacific Railroad terminus in Gerrard to the east. Unfortunately, in the early 1900s the price

Abandoned home along Armstrong Lake

of metals dropped and so did the fortunes of Trout Lake City. Within a few short years the population dropped from over a thousand to just a handful of hardy souls.

One of those that stayed behind was Alice Elizabeth Jowett. She spent over half a century in Trout Lake City. She had left England as a young widow with four children in 1889 and sailed to Vancouver. After a few years in Vancouver she decided Trout Lake City was the place for her. Here she eventually became the owner of the Windsor Hotel. Luxuriously furnished, the stately looking three-story wooden building soon became a rest stop for people visiting from all over the word. It still stands today.

As with most other inhabitants in the area, Alice was not immune to prospecting fever. Soon she had a number of her own claims staked, her favorite being the Foggy Day Mine,

The century-old Windsor Hotel

which we would visit a few days later. Until her late eighties she diligently paid yearly inspection visits to her claims, usually by a combination of horseback and hiking. In her early nineties she insisted in being flown over her claims to view them from above. Despite the virtual death of the rest of Trout Lake City and neighbouring towns, Alice's hotel remained open over the years with spotless table cloths and polished silverware awaiting non-existent guests and a return to the boom times: 'when the boys would come back again'. After more than fifty years in the Lardeau country, age forced her to sell the Windsor Hotel. She eventually moved to a seniors' home in Kelowna where she passed away in 1955 at the age of one hundred and two. Her ashes are buried in the alpine on Silver Cup Ridge, next to the remains of her prospecting cabin, all under the watchful eye of her favorite mine.

As we parked in front of the Windsor Hotel, we noticed that the building was perhaps not as stately-looking as in the pictures from the past. But considering its age, construction – the original foundation consisted of several logs placed on the bare earth – and the extreme snow-loads it had endured annually for over a century, it was in remarkable condition.

After checking in and unloading our bags we were treated to an excellent home cooked meal. During dinner the current owner shared with us some of the hurdles he faced during the multiple restoration phases of the historic building. He was determined and had mastered the art of improvising in an area far from tool rental shops and third-party expertise. After dinner we browsed through the many history books, binders and artifacts on display in the hotel lobby. Pleasantly tired, we climbed the creaky and well-worn staircase to our night's accommodation. According to the cook we would sleep in Alice's bedroom. What an honour! We were the only guests that night.

The next morning we decided on a stroll through the hamlet. The stunning natural beauty of Trout Lake City placed it in a league of its own. If this scenery was in the Swiss Alps it would surely be the exclusive domain of the rich and famous. As it stood, the call of the magnificent peaks, crystal clear waters and quiet isolation tempted only a trickle of newcomers. The century-old framework of streets and blocks of Trout Lake City today lay bare and deserted. The former subdivision properties, first offered for sale in 1894 for $100, or $150 for a corner lot, were covered in grasses and mature tree stands; virtually all original buildings had vanished save the Windsor Hotel.

A group of deer grazed in between former city blocks, uninterested in our presence. They continued their relaxed brunch despite our proximity. Perhaps a prospector charging into town out of the highlands, heralding news of a new mine strike would get their attention. For now they were at home in the town surrounded by mountain silence. Towards the lake and between overgrown lots a few new cabins had been built, randomly spaced and positioned, their builders obviously not confined by restrictive bylaws. Maybe these newcomers would ensure the area's escape from the clutches of ghost town status, the only such Lardeau town fortunate enough to do so.

Century-old gas pump technology

After we bid good-bye to the historic Windsor Hotel we drove to the nearby Trout Lake General Store. This family business has been selling fuel since the 1960s from a set of remarkably preserved gravity-fed pumps, which were moved up from the town site of Burton on Arrow Lake before it was flooded by the dam construction. Talk about a step back in time. If I remember correctly the two pumps were dated 1904 and 1915. No 'pay at the pump service' here. You will need to make the time to first head into the store and introduce yourself to Nancy, the store's owner. Once outside again, Nancy enlightened us with a quick tour and history lesson on early gas pump technology; then I was 'good to go'. I firmly grasped the pump handle with both hands and started to pump the golden mixture from the buried tank beneath my feet into the glass bowl, marked in gallons, above my head, all under Nancy's watchful eye. Then, when I hit the desired fuel level, I stuck the hose nozzle into the vehicle's gas tank and depressed the nozzle lever. Swoosh - no electrons required! Old fashion gravity and physics ensure the gas vacates the pump-mounted glass bowl and ends up in your vehicle's tank. Imagine, the only gas pump for miles that will work during power outages, and no expensive computer parts to replace.

Fascinated by this antiquated but enduring technology, we talked with Nancy for some time before continuing on. Of course we could not miss the cemetery visit that Nancy recommended. We walked around the many overgrown headstones. As judged by the legible grave markers, the Lardeau region provided well for its inhabitants as evidenced by their longevity.

Later we found a secluded camp spot along Trout Lake and took our time setting up our tent and gear for the next few nights. After that we relaxed the day away.

The next morning we met Alan Marlow. The first, and lasting, impression of Alan is that of a true gentleman from simpler times, trustworthy and unhurried. Like many people of his generation, Alan, now in his 80s, is a man whose life of hard work and dedication has directly contributed to the building of Canada. In 1929, at the age of five, Alan emigrated with his family from England to Quebec. From there they crossed Canada by train to Revelstoke and on to Arrowhead, the former rail terminus on the west shore of Arrow Lake. They took a steamer to Beaton, and then caught a ride on the local mail truck to Trout Lake City. He remained here all of his life. To help his family survive during the 1930s depression, Alan started working. There was no time to attend school.

'Had it not been for the fish in the lake we would have had tough times indeed,' he recalled, his British accent still crisp and strong. He proudly displayed an old $20 bill he earned on

Karen and Keera inside an ancient cedar

his first job, at the age of eleven, helping his father fell trees from their land, for use as telegraph poles. Since then, many occupations have graced Alan's resume: mechanic, engineer, logger, road builder, frontiersman, naturalist, rancher, prospector, and surely many more that I am not aware of. Now retired, Alan is still active and always willing to lend a hand. The day we met him he was repairing a vehicle, actually hand fabricating a custom fit part, for a fellow Trout Lake resident. He also works his land, currently establishing a walking trail through an area of amazingly old cedar trees. The 'Staubert Lake Big Cedars', as Alan has named this grove of majestic trees, contains some of the last low-elevation old growth cedar trees in the Kootenays. Alan remarked with great sincerity, 'I have always felt that we should only take what we need from the land'. A tour of the giant cedars on his property is proof of his life long commitment to this principle. The age of one of the smaller trees was measured to be 740 years; the age of the larger trees is estimated at a phenomenal 1900 years.

Standing next to one of these behemoths, touching it, stretching your neck, vainly trying to visually grasp the entire tree at once, you feel honour and shame. It was an honour to be in the presence of living organisms, all of which were already mature trees before Christopher Columbus even set foot on the Americas; some were seedlings shortly after Christ walked on earth. A living plant this old makes our time on earth seem so ridiculously small. I felt shame that since the advent of European presence on this continent, we have virtually eliminated these symbols of time and longevity from our part of the planet. Alan, with an incredulous expression, mentioned that various parties have approached him and suggested turning these last surviving giant cedars into sawmill products as well. 'What good are they just standing there?' they ask him. I cannot help but agree with Alan: why is our species so bent on converting all natural life into short-term profits?

The following day Karen and I searched for an access road, known as the Copper Queen Road – or, as the locals refer to it, the Ruedebeau – which provides four-wheel drive access to one of the most scenic and historic alpine ridges in the Kootenay districts. The Old Reliable, Silver Cup, Polar Star and Last Chance were a few of the nearly fifty mine claims listed as of 1901 on the Silver Cup Ridge. Many of these old mine sites were linked by a prospector path, which now is marked by cairns and signs. There is no continuous vehicular access along this path and ridge, so please, refrain from leaving the trail, as the alpine meadows are very fragile. Unfortunately, some previous motorized visitors have been careless in crossing these meadows. There are also no designated campsites, so if you stay overnight make sure you practice no trace camping.

We left Highway 31 and, after some route finding, started to cross water bar after water bar. We watched the hood of our truck rise and fall countless times, like a small boat on the open sea. Eventually we came to a small trail through a cut block, which we followed until the forest shade swallowed us up. For several kilometres this hairline path wound itself with moderate steepness through dense timber, switch-backing gently to the alpine. We enjoyed bird's-eye views of the valley lakes.

On the last section of trail, before reaching the ridge, a high clearance four-wheel drive was mandatory; the road was steep and narrow, with loose shale and rocks, and inadequate traction would prove disastrous. A promenade of daisies, fireweed and orange tiger lilies championed our climb along this last section. Our arrival on the ridge road was celebrated by a sudden fierce hailstorm. Patiently, we sat inside our cab, while Nature's fury blew all around us, shaking and buffeting our exposed little truck on all sides. We suddenly felt alone and vulnerable in this part of the high country, thankful to have at least some protection from the violent storm. Finally the winds and snow pellets subsided and we felt safe to explore on foot.

Despite the cold mountaintop temperatures and wind gusts, Keera was immediately rolling in deep snow patches, still abundant in shady tree wells. Frisky and overjoyed to be out of the back of the truck, she barked at us, challenging us to throw snowballs for her. She must have been a Husky in a former life.

We explored along the ridge path to the east and the west but the constant cloud cover and roaming storm cells often reduced our visibility to near zero, and kept our hiking to less than a few hours. After eating lunch inside our vehicle, we

En-route to Silver Cup Ridge

headed back down to our lakeside camp.

That night we had an early dinner. Intermittent showers sent us to our tent early, where we snuggled into our warm sleeping bags. Above us whispering winds and light raindrops played in the tree canopy, lulling us to sleep.

Sunshine greeted us early in the morning. We decided to return to Alan's home and join him on his visit to his mining claim near the Silver Cup Ridge, close to Alice's Foggy Day claim. At Alan's cabin we loaded up the chainsaws and headed east on Highway 31, turning onto Rady Creek FSR. The road immediately started to gain elevation. Near the end of a steep clear-cut, a tiny trail veered hard right and uphill, and promptly vanished into deep timber. 'Better lock the hubs here,' Alan grinned, performing a two point turn to get his little four-wheel drive facing skyward up the old passage.

The relatively easy grade of the logging road was now replaced with a punishing steep and narrow trail. This was a classic mining road whose builders, in all likelihood the miners themselves, had only one goal: get to the top as fast as possible. Switchback after switchback, the route drew us closer to Alan's mine and a promise of the wildflower-covered highlands. Looking into the surrounding jungle-like wilderness, with moss covered windfall and boulders rendered half dark by the dense fir and hemlock, I became lost in thought. Here we were, slowly driving up this century-old track in our modern four-wheel drive. A hundred years earlier the miners had climbed this exact trail. I could see them now. Several men breathing heavily, up since before the dawn, their stained leather hats pushed back, their thick flannel shirts and suspenders damp from physical effort. Wearily swatting flies, they called out occasional instructions to one another as they accompanied the thirty-horse pack-train on every step of the path, taking supplies up to the high elevation mine. If the deadfall did not prove too numerous and the horses – and the miners themselves – remained injury free, they would arrive at their destination by dusk. Otherwise they would be forced to travel though the night.

I suddenly had newfound respect for the lode miners of Lardeau's yesteryear. These men who had first ventured into the primeval forests and braved raging rivers, severe climates, ravenous insects and countless more hardships than I was currently, or would I ever be, aware of, sitting in the comfort of my climate controlled cab, could only be described by three words: tough, tough, tough. And after exploring through uncharted territory for months or years, fighting loneliness and depression, always encouraging themselves that the 'big find' was imminent, these very men, if indeed they struck pay dirt, had to build this trail by hand, one axe swing at a time, one shovel load at a time. This route took months to carve out of the virgin terrain. Then they had to carry all supplies and equipment necessary to operate the hard rock mine, not to mention the tons of ore that had to be carried to the valley bottom for processing. Packhorses and men required an entire day to complete this trek in one direction. We would drive up and down it in a matter of hours, and, if it were not for the overburden of fallen trees, without even raising our heart rate. How ridiculously easy our lives were now!

My thoughts broke as Alan backed up to navigate another particularly tight turn. Because of the steep grade, exiting the vehicle to deal with deadfall required keeping the door forced open, a bruised shin or knee would otherwise be your reminder.

Alice's cabin of today

Countless times we stopped and Alan bucked up large deadfall while I hauled the pieces over the trail shoulder. My admiration for Alan escalated to the stratosphere. I knew plenty of men a half century younger than Alan who would not even consider driving up a trail of this nature, much less consider handling a screaming chainsaw to remove downed trees along its course. Karen joked repeatedly that Alan must have found

Alice's cabin of yesterday

the fountain of youth. I honestly believed he had.

We stopped next to a tree, one out of thousands that we had passed, and thousands more to come. Alan pointed: 'My brother scratched the elevation into this tree in the sixties while on horseback'. I could make out 5000 and several feet. 'Still 2000 feet to go,' Alan chuckled as he let out the clutch, and carried us onwards to the heavens. The whine of the transmission in low gear was clearly audible above the engine, a futile protest against the continued steep ascent we were imposing upon it. This trail was much steeper with tighter turns than yesterday's Copper Queen trail.

We arrived at a fork and parked in a tiny clearing on an incline, blocking the wheels with rocks. From here we hiked into a large alpine bowl and down to Alice's memorial cairn. Mrs. Jowett's final resting-place was nestled next to a brook, near her flattened log cabin, a final reminder of her joyous prospecting days in the mountains she loved so much.

As we looked up at the Foggy Day Mine we could make out the mine entrance standing guard above Alice's ashes: a precarious climb far above tree line, along a series of rocky ledges almost vertically above us. The meadow and ridge were ablaze with countless flowers and the storm clouds of yesterday were thankfully lacking today. I sensed that Alice's spirit still lived in these rugged alpine peaks, a fitting resting place for a true Lardeau legend.

Alan's reminiscing was timely; he mentioned chopping wood in the deep winters for Alice as a teenager and being paid $0.25,

Foggy Day Mine Ridge

'a lot of money back then', and how her friendliness and truthfulness touched everyone she met and many whom she never met. We continued our hike up to Alan's claim. As we crested the eastern ridge, our intrusion was announced by an eagle's cry. Visible as a far off black dot in the sky to the east, the

117

Prospecting with Alan

eagle had spotted us and immediately announced our presence to all others in the local animal kingdom. I had no idea that these large raptors would soar so far above the valley floors. Perhaps marmots and gophers inhabiting these areas were the reason for its lofty location. It flew off and we didn't hear or see it again. Perhaps it was unhappy with all the 'traffic'.

Once above the tree line we hiked ever higher. We stumbled over rock fields devoid of all plant life; only brightly coloured fungi survived here. Alan remarked repeatedly how absent-minded of him it was to leave for his mine without changing out of his leather soled street shoes. However, it was impossible for Karen and I, who were wearing hiking boots and whose combined age was less than Alan's, to keep up with him. He seemed to float over the rock fields. With our lungs burning, Karen gasped that Alan had an easier time because he knew the route. What route? We were climbing a huge rock pile. Even nimble Keera was challenged to keep up with this veteran of the mountains, often stopping, contemplating as she gazed over her shoulder down the mountain side, her tongue hanging sideways, surely questioning our sanity between incessant panting.

Long-forgotten mine equipment

Higher still we climbed, our position now above the Foggy Day, which was due west of us. My GPS indicated that we were over 7000 feet in elevation. Breathless, I stopped to take in the

119

panoramic views, truly feeling on top of the world: below us glacier clad mountains, snow-covered cliffs and jumbled masses of rock towered above the dense green canopies, which in turn covered the deep canyons and valley floors. Simultaneously in sight were the Lardeau Range, Bad Shot Range and Goat Range Mountains, and many more I could not name. I briefly felt the desire to grab onto a railing to help steady myself at this height.

Alan's mine had been extensively worked prior to his ownership, as evidenced by large slag piles we passed once we arrived at his claim. Rocks of brilliant and varied patterns lay everywhere, obviously removed from a vein deep within the shafts. Two adits were barely visible, blocked by fallen rock. Following Alan's directions we scoured the piles, breaking rocks, looking for signs of galena. Whenever we found a promising specimen, it was passed to Alan. After an hour of snooping and hammering, Alan's specimen bag was bulging. It was time to pick our way back down to the tree line. With the added weight of the rock bag he was carrying, Alan's speed was finally closer to our own.

We descended the saddle to the east and Alan showed us to another mine, deserted since the 1930s. He mentioned that the owners had purchased a new camp stove. Shortly after its installation, it caused the camp buildings to catch fire and burn to the ground. The buildings were never rebuilt and the mine was abandoned. A mining cart, still patiently awaiting its owners, was perched on narrow gauge rails just outside the mine entrance. A pick axe once held by strong and determined hands now lay discarded inside it. It was nice to see that souvenir hunters had not discovered these mining relics.

We returned to the truck. Alan turned us around on the narrow opening and pointed us downhill. Gravity and the lack of deadfall shortened our return time. With a fresh coat of dust and our adventurer's spirit satisfied we emerged onto Highway 31, and followed it to Alan's home. We shared several pots of tea, far too many ginger cookies, and more fascinating tales of the Lardeau pioneers. Dusk reminded us to bid our farewell to Alan.

Back at our campsite we enjoyed a hearty meal in front of our campfire. The evening was cool and clear as we sat beneath the countless twinkling stars of the milky-way – why settle for a mere five star accommodation? Tired from the day's activities we soon found ourselves in our sleeping bags.

In Reflection...

That last night I lay inside our tent, hands folded behind my head, my mind calm, my body pleasantly tired. I stared into the darkness. The hypnotic waters of nearby Trout Lake slapped the shoreline rocks and tree roots. Outside, Keera, already deep asleep beside a large cedar, groaned contently as she adjusted herself. My whole body glowed with a sense of well being, brought on by the invigorating hike through the mountain air. In my mind I savoured the marvellous experiences of that day, and the past several days since starting on our trip. The mating eagles' dance, the Incomappleux River half-bridge, the legend of Alice Jowett and the ancient Staubert Lake Big Cedars; all had uniquely blessed our backroad journey. The history in the Lardeau was more vivid and alive than in many other parts of BC that we had visited, Nature more untouched. The remoteness and lack of modern amenities in the region had slowed and even resisted change. And perhaps that was not a bad thing. Above all, I felt grateful that we had crossed paths with Alan Marlow's path. The Lardeau, as well as Canada, were blessed to have a pioneer as benevolent and generous as Alan. It was then that I realized I had met a living legend of the Lardeau.

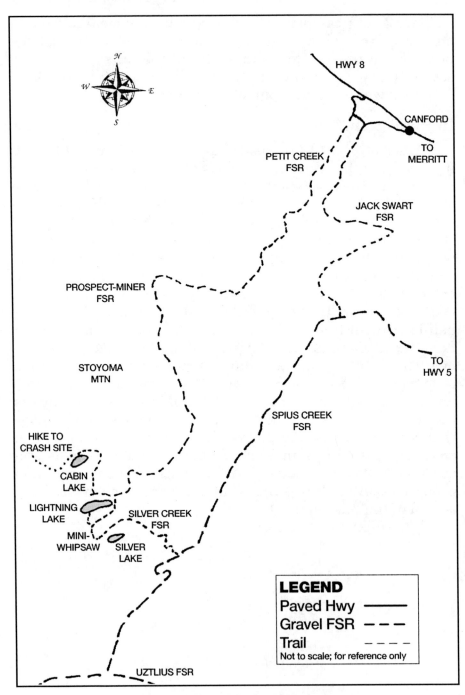

STOYOMA MOUNTAIN LOOP

A Mountain of Tribute

This chapter is dedicated to the men and women who risk their lives fighting forest fires.

...we stopped, caught our breath and looked up. The scene was raw and surreal.

In the Beginning...

The year is 1974. It is a clear Sunday morning on August 11th. In the province of BC it is peak forest fire season. Over 1300 burns have been battled by exhausted fire crews so far this year. The season shows no sign of improvement. In Abbottsford, Eric Yuill, a pilot for Conair Aviation, walks across the tarmac to his waiting water bomber. It has been a black week for Conair. The company lost two planes and four aircrew members in the past eight days while fighting forest fires in southern BC. Eric's assigned plane is a WWII vintage twin engine US Air Force A26 Invader. His water bomber, as other WWII bombers currently in service fighting fires, has been converted to drop fire retardant on burning forests. Eric's task for the day is to ferry the Invader to the air tanker base in Williams Lake, approximately a one-hour flight.

At 8:44 am Eric soars into the air. He levels his craft over the Fraser River and follows it inland. Perhaps his thoughts are with his fellow pilots who were lost earlier that week. The river's course will lead him to his day's destination. The initial weather forecast was favourable for flying. Now the weather has suddenly turned. At 10:04 am the rescue co-ordination centre is notified that Eric is overdue. At 1:00 pm an air search commences with six aircraft. They return at day's end with no results. On Monday, fourteen aircraft participate in the search, again with no results. Day after day the search craft take to the skies. They can find no trace of the missing airman or his machine in the rugged mountainous terrain along the Fraser Canyon. Not until Friday, August 16th, after over 300 hours of searching is the plane discovered. It crashed into the heavily forested Stoyoma Mountain at the 6500 foot level fifteen miles east of Boston Bar.

Eric Yuill was fifty years old. He left behind his wife Jean and four children at home in Summerside, PEI.

As an Okanagan Valley resident who lived through the 2003 Okanagan Mountain Firestorm, which completely destroyed 300 homes, I have ample reason to appreciate the efforts of fire fighters. With my own eyes I experienced the raging fire devouring everything in its path. The sight literally put the fear of God into me. A firestorm is an event so terrifying that without personal experience the feeling of helplessness it imparts to all living beings in its path cannot possibly be portrayed. The men and women at the front lines who combat these infernos, whether on the ground or in the air, are all heroes.

As thanks to these courageous individuals I felt compelled to dedicate a sign of my appreciation by placing a 30th anniversary memorial plaque at the remote crash site of Eric Yuill's plane. My desire is to commemorate Eric and all those persons that have lost their lives fighting forest fires.

On the Trail...

I obtained detailed topographical maps of the area and scoured them. I had only a vague idea of Eric's crash location. Success on finding the crash site would depend on good weather for hiking, a visual sighting, and above all, good luck. Even if we did not find the exact wreckage location we would still place the plaque in the general area.

Joining us on this trip would be Greg Sue. This gentleman is probably one of the best-known four-wheelers in BC, especially to internet-savvy backroaders. His web sites, designed and built by himself, are based on his personal experiences concerning backroad travel by truck and quad, for which Greg has an obvious infectious passion. His web pages played no small part in my devotion to backroad exploration. His sites are examples of the most visited of their kind, eliciting e-mails from around the globe, apparently igniting or fuelling the desire in others to explore backroads and history.

Greg, stout and stocky in frame, has the heart of a lion. It is common knowledge that he has attached his winch cable or tug strap to countless different bumpers, hours from home, often in the middle of the night, regardless of weather conditions.

Crossing an unnamed FSR bridge

Close friend or complete stranger, Greg's time and helping hands are available to anyone. I worked on a particularly difficult vehicle recovery with Greg that took 13 continuous hours. Greg, whose truck was left with bent sheet metal and broken fixtures, turned down all remuneration, all for a stranded backroader he had never met before. There are few people more dependable and level headed than Greg to have as a companion when exploring remote country trails.

We left the Okanagan Valley with temperatures reading 37C and welcomed the much cooler air on the higher elevation mountain highways until we descended into the Nicola Valley. In Merritt, we topped our gas tanks to the limits and quickly hit the road, eager to once again leave the hot arid temperatures behind.

Twenty kilometres west of Merritt, with Karen and myself in the lead, we turned onto Petit Creek FSR. We passed ranch homes along the way as we snaked high above the canyon of Spius Creek. At one point in Prospect Creek Canyon, we admired towering rock sculptures on the steep slopes above the road, the artistic accomplishments of time and erosion. We crossed a bridge and stayed left on the Prospect-Miner FSR. The elevation gains were now impressive and allowed sweeping views to the southeast hillsides.

Several kilometres after a small bridge, we took a trail to the right and uphill. This was the original sheep trail into Cabin Lake. We engaged four-wheel drive for the remaining kilometres. Once around a cut block the timbers enveloped us and the trail became more challenging; numerous washouts, gullies and loose shale on steep climbs demanded the driver's attention.

As we crested the final hill before Cabin Lake I noticed a long grassy, and unusually wide, trail running due south. It provoked my curiosity as we left it wayside. Straight ahead we started a sharp descent. To our right, blackened tree trunks stood silent, like gigantic shrivelled matchsticks, victims of a century old fire. Down to our left, like a shimmering carpet in the setting sun, Cabin Lake appeared.

There was no odour of smoke, no man made colours hidden amongst the virgin wood on the small peninsula, no movement of any kind. We alone intruded upon silence. Slowly we drove the narrow trail into our night's hidden habitation, past the lake's namesake, a small deserted log cabin. Its door rested on a single leather hinge, its sod roof had partly collapsed and its single window opening stared blankly at the lake. Evidence of the shepherd's time spent here accompanying his flock throughout the summer, now consisted of an old rusted wood stove lying on its side in front of the cabin. Many quiet memories lay

Heading to Cabin Lake

forgotten within the crumbling walls of this cabin. This shelter kept its secrets well as it waited patiently and peacefully through all the decades for the return of another caring owner. Now neglected and forsaken it sat in quiet decay, certainly

127

aware that a final and merciless winter snow would soon level it completely. My gaze returned to the lake.

We parked, stretched our legs, and slowly walked the perimeter of this beautiful jetty. I had visited numerous alpine

Cabin Lake and Stoyoma Mountain

lakes nestled in this sort of tranquil solitude. Yet Cabin Lake felt unique, a cut above, in fact – exclusive. I could not put my finger on it at first, but for those that believe and sense energy from such places I would call it unusually 'Powerful'. Surely this lake deserved a far more majestic name than Cabin Lake.

I would learn the next day the reason for this special energy oasis that I felt.

It was now after 8:00 pm. Karen and I set up our tent and Greg started cutting up the firewood he had gathered. For some reason I took a particular interest in the wood, noticing that they were all long slim poles, unlike the usual assortment of tree debris lying around the forest floor. It was then that I realized that Greg had inadvertently collected the scattered poles that were meant as the wooden frame supports of a tepee. Judging by the shape and length of the poles, they had been transported in from outside the area. We decided to bundle them together and lean them up against a tree, hoping to prevent further firewood confusion for other campers.

No sooner had we started the campfire than the unmistakable thump of helicopter rotors echoed through our tiny hidden valley. I sighed. At times it seems impossible to escape manmade sounds. The helicopter appeared high above, repeatedly circling our camp spot. Greg and I looked at each other with the same thought: maybe a camp fire ban was in effect! I had checked the Forestry web page prior to our departure, which indicated no ban in this area. Eventually the big bird put down several hundred feet west of us in a small meadow.

'Talk about taking the easy way up' Karen laughed. After the craft had shut down, four passengers emerged. They carried a large white cross and started to walk away from us into the forested edge of the meadow. The pilot stayed behind with the helicopter. Relieved that we were not to be cited for a Forestry infraction I made my way over to chat with the airman. The gentleman, perhaps in his early sixties, explained that the passengers had charted his craft and asked to land somewhere on Stoyoma Mountain. Here they wished to spread the ashes of their parents and pay tribute to them. The parents had spent many wonderful seasons hunting and exploring here throughout their long lives. Apparently Stoyoma Mountain had been chosen by others as well, to symbolize a mountain of tribute.

When I inquired whether the pilot knew of the Invader crash site, he mentioned that he had actually worked as a mechanic for Conair in the 1960s and knew of Eric, but had not met him. He knew of the crash but did not know exactly where it lay. None-the-less I found it a strange coincidence. I thanked him and headed back to camp. The helicopter lifted off with much wind and noise and we were again the sole inhabitants of beautiful and quiet Cabin Lake.

That night around the campfire, we took our ringside seats to enjoy a rare treat of Nature – the rise of a blue moon (a blue moon is when a full moon occurs twice in one month). Large and full, it slowly took up the entire night sky. Bright enough to read by, the moon gently emerged over the eastern ridge, illuminating countless evergreen silhouettes. Occasionally an owl hooted from deep within the shadows, temporarily drowning out the crackling embers and our conversation. Despite the daytime heat, the high elevation caused temperatures to plummet to near freezing that night. We put on our heavy sweaters. When our wood supply exhausted we retired to our sleeping bags. I relished the absolute quiet as I fell asleep.

I awoke at first light the next morning, unusually refreshed. My first thoughts were to find the plane wreckage. As I quietly prepared to depart, Karen awoke and decided to join me. We agreed to leave Greg asleep in the back of his truck.

As the first sunrays crept into our small basin and reflected off the lake's surface we followed a narrow trail along the shore. Countless flying insects hummed above the placid waters, circling, dive-bombing and chasing one another; Cabin Lake inhabitants were early risers. After a steep climb, we came upon a hiking trail that headed west into the high mountains. There was no sign of recent bear activity but we kept our conversation to a maximum to broadcast our presence. After several hours, during which we stopped countless times, searching the surroundings with binoculars and squinted eyes, our search for any trace of human made materials or colours proved futile. Disappointed and tired, I realized that the vast and heavily forested sides of Stoyoma Mountain would not reveal their secrets easily. We, in fact, were searching for the proverbial needle in a haystack. Thirsty and hungry we agreed to turn around.

As a sign of defiance, I lifted the binoculars one final time and there it was! The wreckage was several kilometres due west of us, glistening in the morning sun. It sat at the halfway-point up a steep rocky slope below a small grove of evergreens in a large alpine bowl. Elated, and surprised at our blind luck, I called out to Karen. I scoured the wreck further but could not define any parts at our distance, even with binoculars. Had the sun been absent that day, the crash site would not have made itself known to us; we noted the co-ordinates and turned back to camp.

During breakfast with Greg we decided to take advantage of the superb weather and planned a hike to the crash site in the late afternoon. We anticipated the hike would require four hours; this morning's section of the hike was an intermediate skill level, the section further up was likely more advanced.

Just after 3:00 pm Greg, Karen and I headed back out on the trail, with Keera in the lead. We made good time, even though we were loaded down with water canteens, snacks, the memorial plaque and tools. The trail showed signs of recent clearing, but in most places it was just wide enough for a single person. At regular intervals I noticed old blaze marks scarring large tree trunks. Past the initial morning viewpoint we now descended into a swampy plateau, speckled with stunted trees and pockets of dense brush. The mosquitoes and black flies immediately became more aggressive. We increased our pace, despite the sweat that was running down our temples and backs, staining our caps and T-shirts. When we stopped to drink from the canteen, clouds of vicious mosquitoes instantly surrounded us. Greg appeared to have a natural lure for the bothersome fliers.

Finally, we broke out of the marsh area and the mountain breeze helped keep the insects at bay. The plane lay a kilometre ahead across an open meadow and halfway up the steep basin wall. We picked our way across the uneven ground, tripping and stumbling, our eyes glued to the scattered pieces of silver randomly strewn across the steep rockslide.

Eventually we reached the edge of the meadow; swamp

131

grasses gave way to rock up the north-facing ridge of the bowl. We stopped, caught our breath and looked up. The scene was raw and surreal. Here, the outer perimeter of the debris field started. At our feet lay torn and unrecognisable pieces of all sizes, shapes and colours, likely carried down by rain and snow

Greg beside the Conair cockpit

over the last three decades. The ravages of time appeared non-existent on the plane's exterior. The aluminium plane finish looked just as shiny as it surely did the day it rolled off the assembly line during WWII.

Ascending this section of rock proved much steeper than we had anticipated, even from the meadow's edge. We were forced to crawl on hands, knees and feet for all of the distance. In order to judge our direction and progress, we were obliged to stop crawling, stand partially upright with one hand still touching the ground, and cautiously lean our head far back onto our neck to see up extreme slope above us; all the while concentrating on maintaining our balance and fighting off bouts of vertigo. Needless to say progress was slow.

Upon impact the plane had broken into three main discernible sections: the fuselage had folded itself under the cockpit, the Conair insignia still clearly legible on the nose of the craft; one engine lay on its own with the bent and mangled

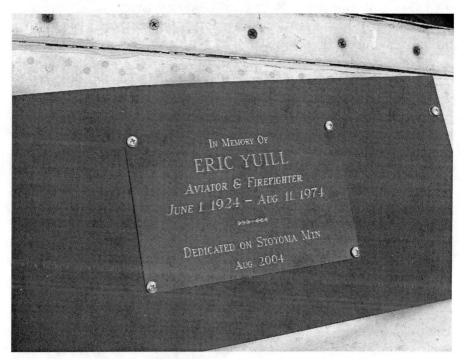

Eric Yuill memorial plaque

propeller still attached; the other was literally engulfed by the twisted wing structure that had inconceivably wrapped itself around the engine like a blanket. There was no sign of any fire or smoke damage. Throughout the debris field lay thousands of bent and mangled aircraft pieces, ranging from screws and bolts to landing gear and tires. The cockpit had all instrumentation panels removed, either by souvenir hunters or perhaps by the initial crash investigation team.

During the next hour we cautiously moved about the crash site. Then we rested and viewed the wreck from the small grove of trees above the scene. We sat in silence, thankful for the protection from the sun. The beauty of the cloudless, hot summer day was in stark contrast to the deadly carnage at our feet. The steep walls of the alpine bowl formed a near complete circle around us; only a small flat valley to the southeast led into this isolated area. Was that the way Eric had entered almost thirty years ago to the day, only to realize that the bowl he was in had ridges too steep to climb, even for his powerful machine? We sat in our own thoughts, no one wanting to speak. The only sounds were Keera panting and an occasional slap as we defended ourselves against persistent black flies that had followed us from the grasses. A welcomed breeze bathed our bodies as it swept up from the valley floor. The day was starting to cool. Then someone broke the silence. It was getting late. The sun had dropped behind the western ridge and we would have to double-time our hike back to avoid being caught by nightfall on the trail. We picked a path back down to the cockpit. After attaching the plaque, we sent a few final thoughts and thanks.

Several hours later, drenched in sweat, and with aching feet, we arrived back at Cabin Lake. To maximize the remaining daylight hours we hiked back without breaks. We now had neighbours; a Native family from the Nicola Valley was camping next to us.

That night one of the men, Jerry, spent time with us at our camp fire. He shared with us the Native history of the beautiful mountain lake. For countless generations, Native tribes had come from the surrounding valleys at this time of year to trade and socialize at the tiny lake. It was then known as Goat Lake, named after a herd of mountain goats that made their home in the basin. He informed us that the trail we hiked earlier that day was an ancient Native trail. It continued across the mountain ridges and into the Fraser Canyon; this accounted for the old blaze marks I had seen on the trees. The long straight trail at the top of Cabin Lake that we had noticed upon our arrival was known as the Raceway. Here, braves would challenge one another to race horses along its wide corridor, with their families camped in tepees along each side of the route, cheering them on, hooting and hollering. The only tribe members allowed on the small peninsula that we were currently camped on were the Shaman. These were the medicine men of the Native tribes, who wielded great power and authority. While the rest of the community was celebrating along the Raceway, the Shaman performed spiritual rituals on the peninsula. Jerry indicated that due to the high number of Shaman present during the generations of gatherings the effect of the medicine practised here was unusually potent and long lasting. For decades after the last of these ceremonies occasional Native visitors to this basin still expressed that they felt a sense of lingering energy, at times spooking man and horse. The annual Native gatherings eventually became less frequent; the Potlatch Law, which made it illegal for Natives to gather in numbers for any reason, was enforced in varying degrees over its time from 1884 through 1951. (Natives traditionally held potlatches as a tribe or small group for ceremonial purposes, to feast and distribute gifts. In the 1800s the Dominion – or Federal Government – enacted legislation prohibiting the act of engaging in potlatches, punishable by imprisonment.)

Jerry remembered, as a small child, one of the last secret gatherings here at the Racetrack in the late 1930s. At that time the entire Cabin Lake area, except for the peninsula, was without tree cover. It had recently been devoured by a forest fire; hence the old blackened tree trunks we noticed upon our arrival. The cabin we passed had not yet been built. It was erected by sheepherders after the tribes were no longer permitted to gather here. The mountain goats then disappeared too; the sheep herds introduced in the 1940s and 1950s proved too numerous, their voracious appetites leaving little for the local wildlife to consume.

Jerry told us the tepee poles we had come across were more than likely used by the Shaman, possibly quite old, and thanked us for placing them aside. His family and friends still camped here annually to pay tribute to the generations that had met here before them. As our campfire started to die, Jerry excused himself and headed back to his own camp.

The next day dawned bright and clear. After a late breakfast we took our time and explored around the lake. On the way to the Raceway we visited the cross placed by the helicopter visitors two days before. We walked over a small creek and climbed up to the south end of the ancient Raceway. We wandered along its length and imagined the cheering spectators lining the causeway with painted tepees as a backdrop. We could almost see the dust fly and feel the ground shake as horses and riders charged to the finish line, the inevitable joy and disappointment to follow, only to be forgotten by the next round of competition. This stretch of trail certainly harboured exciting events of times past.

Back at camp we let the ambience of our surroundings soothe us. After yesterday's arduous hike we deserved a rest. We spent the day talking, reading, napping and just being with Nature. After dinner, bedtime came early for us; thankfully our neighbours were exceptionally considerate and quiet.

The next morning Jerry waved good-bye as he and his family left. We made sure we had practised no trace camping and then pointed our dusty trucks uphill, leaving the cabin and lake in the care of the mountain spirits.

We chose the route to Lightning Lake, and after a tailgate lunch, took a challenging trail several kilometres east of the lake. After passing through overgrown trail sections we emerged several kilometres above Silver Lake. Just before a creek crossing we were forced to a halt. A spruce grouse was certain we were trespassing on 'its' road and would not move an inch as it stared down our truck. Indignant, it let out a series of peeping clucks, determined to have us turn around. Every conceivable vocal sound that we dreamt up, horn blowing or inching our truck closer did not faze our stoic contender. It held its ground.

Spruce grouse are found throughout dense coniferous forests in BC, other than on the coast. They often show little or no fear of man and are sometimes called 'fool hens' for this very

Trailside life

reason. This particular fellow was certainly a cut above other grouse we had met so far on the trailside. Finally he forced my hand and I was obliged to climb out of the truck and escort him up the embankment. Even then he made his way in an unhurried and belligerent manner. I just know he laughed at me as I ran back to our vehicle to quickly vacate the road before he returned to re-challenge us.

After carefully crossing a precarious tiny bridge which was missing the middle deck sections, we continued down the Silver Lake FSR until we joined the Spius Creek FSR. Here we turned north, arriving at the Jack Swart FSR turn off. This scenic old trail was the slow and bumpy route into Merritt. It had become even slower and bumpier thanks to the addition of countless water bars on the trail. If you have the time, this old trail is a true joy to drive, granting views deep into the Stoyoma

Mountain area and the Spius Creek Canyon, as it slowly meanders, literally within touching distance, of giant old growth Ponderosa Pines. Your four-wheel drive skills will also enjoy the workout.

Our exit point onto Highway 8 was near Canford, the site of an abandoned railway storage yard for the Nicola Valley Company Sawmill built there in 1908. The sawmill was large and profitable enough to afford to lay a train track, called the Canford Spur. It was built along the western side of Spius Creek,

Man and dog, tired after a long day

down which the large timbers could be floated from the higher elevations and then loaded onto the railcars for transport to the hungry mill.

In Merritt we topped our empty fuel tanks. After filling our tummies at our favourite family diner, the Home Restaurant on Voght Street, we headed home tired and content.

138

In Reflection...

After visiting Stoyoma Mountain I was unsure if I would publish a chapter on it. My concern was the potential adverse effect on the delicate balance at beautiful Cabin Lake and the surrounding area. Could it survive a potential increase of backroad explorers, whether in trucks or on ATV's? And what of the Invader crash site? Would souvenir hunters eventually carry off all parts, leaving no sign of Eric Yuill's memorial? All valid concerns.

I feel, however, there is a responsibility to be shared by those with the knowledge of such places to help provide opportunities to others, to ensure that more people become involved with protecting, repairing, and helping preserve for future generations our wilderness areas. By getting more people actively enjoying the mountains, sympathetic to the preservation of the environment and the history they have personally experienced, or have read about, the public will become more proactive to police itself.

Stoyoma Mountain, as evidenced by its solitary beauty, its Native heritage and Eric Yuill's memorial site, is a sacred place. If you do visit this area please treat it with the utmost respect, as it truly is a mountain of tribute for many.

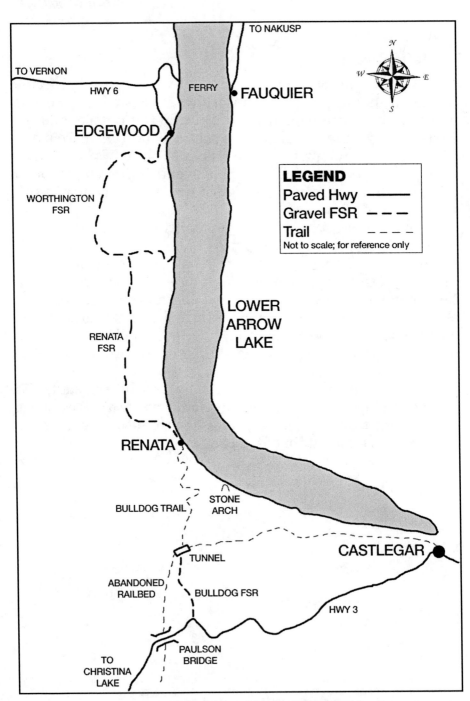

BULLDOG TRAIL - HWY 3 TO HWY 6

Bulldog Biter

...we now navigated many kilometres back down to the lake, and into the comforts of a welcoming hamlet...or so we thought.

In the Beginning...

Bulldog Mountain sits at the southern end of Lower Arrow Lake in the West Kootenays. From its peak, your view extends from Granby Provincial Park in the west to the Purcell Mountains in the east. The Bulldog Mountain Traverse is a great four-wheel drive adventure that allows backroad travel from the Paulson Pass on Highway 3, north, to the village of Edgewood, just off Highway 6. Allow two days or more for a comfortable trip. Inexperienced drivers will become experienced drivers. Experienced drivers will be challenged by trail clearing and spotting for companion vehicles. Everyone will enjoy the views, Nature and history en-route.

Depending on the trail conditions, lower clearance four-wheel drive vehicles may become hung up and require a buddy vehicle with pull strap to get them moving again. Do not leave without a chainsaw or a large friend with a sharp hand saw. I have never crossed this pass without encountering numerous deadfall on the trail. This trip includes old rail bed travel, a railway tunnel, an assassination memorial, abandoned towns, a 100-year old mine, a secluded waterfall and a wide variety of four-wheel drive terrain.

Access to Bulldog Mountain can be gained from east of the Paulson Pass Bridge by turning onto the abandoned railway bed. Another option is to continue past the bridge for several kilometres and turn onto the Bulldog FSR. Stay left until a yellow gate is reached at the 22km marker. A small trail leads up to the mountain peak and down the other side into the remnants of the town of Renata. From there the trail fords Renata Creek and then becomes Renata FSR, a high elevation logging road. Weather permitting it grants impressive mountain views into the Valhallas.

When we first drove this trail it was my initial experience with a multiple-day backroad trip. As I discovered after becoming lost and running out of fuel and provisions, I had not properly planned for it. In fact, it is fair to say that I was one of those inexperienced drivers that became a lot more experienced after this trip.

On the Trail...

Our weekend travel group consisted of two vehicles: Kari and Lucy in their 4Runner and Karen and I, along with our dog Keera, in our truck. We arrived at the Paulson Bridge around noon and struck for the historic rail line, originally built as the Columbia and Western in 1897 and later purchased by the Canadian Pacific Railway in 1911. This stretch of rail line joined the famous Kettle Valley Railway (KVR) in Midway, near Grand Forks. The KVR was built in stages over many years through the southern interior mountain ranges. Once completed, it provided access for an entire generation of British Columbians to the vast natural resources of the Kootenay regions. This now-abandoned railway provides much enjoyment to hikers, mountain bikers and backroaders. For the fascinating in-depth history of the KVR, I suggest reading the book *McCulloch's Wonder*, by Barrie Sanford.

After lunch at an old campsite, we continued north with Kari in the lead. The smooth rail bed surface made for a leisurely drive with minimal dust. We stopped at the monument, slightly below the rail bed grade, that marked the location of where the Doukhobor leader, Peter 'The Lordly' Verigin, was assassinated. Along with nine other victims, his rail car on a CPR passenger train was ripped apart by a bomb in 1924. It's hard to believe that even in the peaceful Kootenays terrorists have plied their trade.

The guilty party was never apprehended. Perhaps the most intriguing aspect of this historic murder mystery has yet to

The Verigin Memorial

unfold. Apparently as recent as the 1990s, and despite numerous requests from researchers, government officials have not released the entire results of their investigation from that time period. A number of conspiracy theories ranging from a government led plot to a Russian assassin have arisen as a consequence.

The Doukhobors, a Russian pacifistic religious group escaping persecution in their homeland, had moved to the BC interior in 1908. Through hard work and communal efforts the Doukhobors became self-sufficient. Within a decade they had cleared thousands of acres of land, planted orchards, built a sawmill and brick and irrigation pipe factories. They became a hub of commerce in the area. However, their success and different communal values caused resentment from the English-speaking communities. After the murder of their charismatic leader things went from bad to worse for the Doukhobors, culminating with the repossession of all their properties by trust and mortgage companies during the depression years of the 1930s.

Today abandoned brick Doukhobor homes from that period are still visible in the Grand Forks area along Highway 3.

Continuing on, we entered the station remains of Farron, named after a railway construction engineer. Farron supplied coal and water for the trains passing through Bulldog Tunnel. Helper locomotives, used to assist the trains pass the steep grades up from the valley, were disconnected or connected here depending on the direction of travel. There were still building foundations and a root cellar to be found amongst the coal-saturated soils that surround Farron. Hundreds of tiny craters make for difficult walking in this area; they were left behind by dedicated treasure hunters brandishing metal detectors and shovels.

We drove on, enjoying the views down onto Dog Creek and across the valley into the Christina Range of the Monashee Mountains, carefully slowing down for the blind corners on the rail bed. We manoeuvred around one last curve and stared into the inky black of the Bulldog Tunnel. Like a huge gateless dungeon the tunnel ominously beckoned. Near the entrance patches of brilliant green mosses and stunted grass clumps, somehow finding hold on vertical surfaces, dotted the glistening walls. While hidden in the shadows small waterfalls splashed over jet-black rock, discoloured from decades of coal fired locomotive exhaust. Inside the tunnel was eerie, and yet beautiful.

The cool dampness in the air and the hollow sound of water echoing from far inside the blackness, added to the fascination of this feat of construction.

The Bulldog Tunnel is nearly 3000 feet in length. Throughout its service life it was the longest tunnel in the southern interior of BC. During the two-year construction period, trains

Bulldog East Entrance

operated over five miles of temporary switchbacks. Some of these switchbacks can still be accessed just past the eastern entrance of the tunnel. An ill-placed gate just before the Bulldog Traverse trailhead restricts travel to the remaining Bulldog FSR section.

I was now in the lead and with slight apprehension, headlights piercing the emptiness, we cautiously rolled into the long curved tunnel with no end in sight. The water echoes were now replaced by the loud crunching of rocks and pebbles under our mud tires. This sound, perpetually amplified through the long hollow, was deafening until we rolled up the windows. As we steered around the large rocks that had crashed down from the walls and ceilings, I stared at the rough-hewn rock surfaces, blasted and smashed out by labourers over a century ago. Not

Inside Bulldog Tunnel

a job for the timid. With utter darkness behind our trucks, I found myself fighting claustrophobia. I thought of the many millions of tons of mountain that were a few feet above our tiny truck cab. Eager to return to daylight, I focussed past the opaque reflections of our headlights, searching for natural light, the reverberating crunch between rocks and tires our only companion. Finally, a fuzzy but distinct beacon of light appeared far ahead. The end was in sight.

Ironically, my claustrophobia suddenly worsened. I struggled to convince myself that our underground passage would not collapse within the next five minutes. Upon exiting the long tunnel the sun felt uncomfortably hot and it momentarily blinded us. I was not complaining.

We followed the rail bed for several kilometres until we faced a washout, forcing us to turn around. We would have to head through the tunnel again. This time, with experience on my side, the drive was less anxious. I even stopped to take a picture, albeit a quick one.

After backtracking on the rail bed, we turned left near two large boulders onto a tiny cart track. The thick undergrowth swallowed us up. This tough trail tested our truck's capabilities; four-wheel drive and a lack of concern for the vehicle's paint finish were imperative to continue. After an hour or more we exited onto the Bulldog FSR and picked a clearing to camp for the night.

It seemed we had just retired to our cozy sleeping bags when in the distance, passing logging trucks rumbled us out of our sleep. This continued throughout the night. We were early risers that morning and a little grumpy. After breakfast, Kari and I scouted ahead in his 4Runner, searching for the Bulldog trailhead. We found the entrance blocked by a large pile of freshly felled trees. Fortunately, one of the heavy logging equipment operators offered to move the pile for us. When we returned several hours later, the path was clear. We switched into four-low gear and started up the trailhead. This trail was the former access road to a Forestry lookout on the peak of Bulldog Mountain. As with most Forestry lookouts, the one on Bulldog had two access routes: one up the north side and one up the south side of the mountain. In case of a forest fire the lookout caretaker might escape down the alternate route.

Riel Marquardt

We would ascend Bulldog from the southern access route and descend down the northern route into the former town of Renata. The trail into Renata is the steeper and more difficult section, so if you feel challenged beyond your comfort level on the southern approach I would recommend not attempting the northern access route. Removal of deadfall was constantly required, and numerous washed out sections demanded several attempts to pass successfully. The grown-in trail took us several hours to navigate, all of it in four-low gear.

Bulldog Lookout Tower

At the summit we were rewarded with a soft cooling wind and endless views in all directions. The only sound was that of our own heartbeats, still invigorated from the trail clearing efforts. What a marvellous but lonely home this must have been for the lookout caretaker, living here in solitude for the summer months of the year. After a scenic tailgate lunch we put the trucks into four-low again.

The night before two men on ATVs had passed by our campsite and emphatically stated, with respect to the northern trail descent into Renata: 'You won't make it down that trail. Not even in those machines!' as they motioned to our lifted trucks. They appeared seasoned riders, and spoke with an air of authority. At the time I had glanced alarmed at Kari, who seemed undisturbed by their certainty. As we now pressed on and started our downward thrust towards Renata, I kept hearing their words. Would the trail become too steep and too narrow for us to turn around on? Would we reach a point of no return?

The tall timbers below the mountain peak surrounded us until we reached Renata. The trail on the north side of the mountain had the taste of an early mining road with its tight switchbacks and challenging grade. I found myself firmly gripping the steering wheel, using it to brace myself, trying to counteract gravity as it forced my torso uncomfortably into my seatbelt. Karen hung onto the passenger handle above her door with one hand, and used the other to brace herself against the glove box. The loose shale and rock made it difficult for our tires to find traction, especially when backing up to navigate the hairpin turns. Any steeper would have been too steep; any narrower would have been too narrow. As on our ascent, our chainsaws often echoed through the deep forest as we were forced to stop and cut away remnants from the windstorms that frequent the area. Sometimes we were faced with one random tree and other times with many trees that formed a tangled mess on the trail ahead of us.

Several kilometres into the descent, the abandoned Mountain Chief Mine appeared. This mine was worked intermittently from 1903 until the 1950s. It produced copper from open trenches and inclined shafts. An aerial tram one kilometre long was constructed in 1919 to haul the ore to Arrow Lake at the mountain bottom, where it awaited shipment to the smelter in Trail. The mine buildings and tram supports were now heaps of wooden rubble with abandoned equipment and steel cable strewn throughout the area. We exercised extreme caution while exploring the abandoned mine site, 'test stepping' with one foot prior to committing our entire body weight in given areas, mindful of the possibility of grown-over ventilation shafts or rotten wood structures buried beneath our feet.

Abandoned Mountain Chief Mine

Past the mine site the Bulldog trail started to lose its bite. Several kilometres before the bridge over Dog Creek hung a small white sign indicating the Renata Waterfall hiking trail, four kilometres in length. The falls were situated at the end of the path, down a steep embankment in a secluded hollow. Water thundered over the smooth grey granite ledges on a back drop of rock walls carpeted in moss, creating an almost spiritual hideaway.

Once back in our trucks we rambled into the outskirts of the remaining buildings of Renata. Three French prospectors founded Renata in 1897. They built a hotel, which they eventually sold to a gentleman called Fred Nash. Fred cleared the land and planted the first orchard. In 1907, a real estate company bought all the land and subdivided it. A large number of Mennonite families moved from the prairies and named the

Renata Waterfall

area Renata. With its mild weather and sheltered location it was ideal for fruit growing; some of the fruit trees survive to this day. During its peak production years thousands of pounds of fruit were picked, packed in wooden boxes built in Renata factories and shipped to points beyond. There was no road into Renata; access was by stern wheeler and later by cable car ferry service.

Renata was one of numerous towns drowned with the damming and subsequent flooding of the Arrow Lakes when the Hugh Keenleyside Dam at Castlegar was completed in mid-summer 1969. This was one of three dams built in a co-operative US-Canadian venture, and the big dollar mega-project paid little attention to the affected residents. They were forced to relocate, their homes and businesses then set ablaze. As the man-made floodwaters were unleashed they crept up and over the charred remains, hiding them forever from sight. Thousands of lives were disrupted, all signs of the past instantly erased by the decisions of a few in offices far away. Move or drown: the price of progress.

Renata Cabin

The Renata of today lies in the hills above the former town site. It consists of a number of hidden summer homes from near-new to run-down, original relocated buildings such as the schoolhouse, assorted trailers and numerous seemingly abandoned vehicles. One feels slightly unsure as to the reception, if any, one should expect from a chance meeting with a local. The quiet in this area is almost too quiet, yet soothing in nature. Upon entering the hamlet, a sense of timelessness gently envelops the visitor.

Renata Post Office

Following Kari, we turned right at the narrow Dog Creek Bridge. A short distance down a well worn track, a man we later came to know as 'George the Wood-Carver' appeared out of the underbrush to greet us. George is the history book image of a mountain man: tall, lean and handsome, with thick blond

153

hair and a matching long beard that rests on his chest. A hardy man of obvious quiet inner strength, he speaks with conviction and dry humour, no matter the topic. He has honest clear eyes, thundering laughter and slight limp when walking. It reveals

Renata Pay Phone

the true grit of this gentleman, who, together with his wife Grace, raised their family in Renata in conditions similar to those of the early Kootenay pioneers. George and his wife were the only year round inhabitants of Renata. Yearning for more elbowroom and an escape from society's confining rules, they left a Vancouver suburb fifteen years earlier. Renata met their requirements perfectly, despite – or perhaps because of – the total lack of modern amenities and reasonable road access. Harvesting cedar wood from his land, George has let his talents as a chainsaw wood carver blossom. His creations can be found at marinas, gift shops, and businesses throughout the interior, his giant chess sets sought after by hotel chains.

George takes his bear carvings to market

After a lengthy and enjoyable chat we parted ways with George, already looking forward to our next visit. Upon our return to the base of Bulldog Mountain our two trucks parted ways as well. Karen and I had to be back at work the next morning. The two of us could not help feel a tinge of envy and sadness as we waved good-bye. Kari pointed the 4Runner back up the narrow ascent to Bulldog's peak; he and Lucy were set for another week off to enjoy more backroad exploring, while the adventure time for Karen and I was quickly drawing to a close... or so we thought!

Now alone, we crossed the Dog Creek Bridge and continued north; ahead lay the Renata Creek crossing and the Renata FSR. In charge of my own navigation, I felt comforted by the fact that I could depend on one thing: my map book. Aware of our plans to separate today, I had studied my 'mighty' map book several nights in a row. It indicated that a small black line, labelled Renata FSR, snaked its way high above the western shore of Arrow Lake from Renata back to pavement at the farming settlement of Edgewood.

'Easy… about 80 kilometres, we'll be there in two hours or less', I thought. We drove to the geographic point of the Renata delta, to exactly where George mentioned the creek crossing should be on our left. Only we could see no sign of a crossing. He had mentioned that he had never driven this way himself, always travelling by boat in and out of Renata. I sat puzzled. The only access to the left was a steep sandy embankment along the lake with ATV tracks. This passage was just wide enough for ATVs, and the lake waters were already licking at the lower tire track.

'No one in their right mind would possibly consider taking his truck along that!' I reassured myself, turning our vehicle around to see where we had erred in direction. Surely we had missed the real access point to the Renata Creek crossing.

One at a time we followed all other branches. They were all dead ends. I felt mild panic set in. I grabbed the CB microphone to summon Kari, who by now was well on his way back up Bulldog Mountain. His radio had not been working well and as I feared, he did not respond. We really were on our own.

Back down to the beach and land point we drove. Turn around and back to all the dead ends. Thoroughly confused, I grabbed my mighty map book; surely it held the answer. But the scale was too large to show any detail within Renata. My mild panic became a full-blown attack: sweaty palms, throbbing temples and a mind that would suddenly not stop racing! How was I to get us out of this place? I was not prepared, nor my truck capable, to drive up the Bulldog trail as Kari's better equipped truck could. I prayed our truck wouldn't join the ranks of the other apparently abandoned vehicles we had noticed, never to leave Renata again. As a budding backroad explorer, on my own for barely an hour and already I had us hopelessly marooned. Was this all I was capable of?

Back down to the beach. I scampered on foot along the sandy embankment and ATV path, hoping my haste would help reveal the answer to the secret of leaving Renata before it was too late. Sure enough, the Renata Creek crossing was on the other side, hidden behind a bend. This discovery briefly eased my anxiety; however, the thought of navigating this steep off-camber embankment, where a rollover would put us on our roof under lake water, made me extremely uncomfortable. My anxiety levels shot to new highs. What other choice did I have?

I dug deep into my shaken explorer's heart, tried to calm my mind and muttered some unintelligible words concerning the motto for all true adventurers, artificially encouraging myself. Keera followed Karen as she climbed out of the truck. I put the transmission into gear, triple checked my four-wheel drive indicator light, and eased the clutch. The embankment section was maybe a hundred feet in length. It only seemed like forever. I held my breath. I could hear my heart pounding. I felt my toes straining on the accelerator pedal. In trepidation, I leaned out my window for extra ballast on the high side of the vehicle, fully aware that it would make little difference. it was my only means of relieving the tension I felt. In extreme slow motion, one tire revolution at a time, I inched across the embankment. Finally, I was back on level hard ground and Renata Creek was in full view. I suddenly felt GREAT! What a RUSH! I sprang out of the truck. Sharing our joy, Karen and I jumped up and down, laughing like children. Even Keera barked, rounding out the chorus.

As our excitement eased, we cast our attention to the creek crossing. A crude ford was in place, but the far embankment looked sudden and jagged. However, in comparison to the previous adventure, the worst case scenario here involved moving some large boulders with a shovel, not a potential vehicle write-off. Armed with a new sense for adventure, I navigated the creek ford, the waters less than a foot deep. Despite getting hung up climbing the far embankment, the truck was soon sitting level again without any manual labour necessary. None-the-less, others are cautioned that during peak runoff times the lake can rise sufficiently and within 24 hours, the embankment route is flooded and traps vehicles on the eastern side for extended time periods.

As we headed up the narrow Renata FSR trail it was well past dinnertime, only a few hours of daylight remained. 'Maybe

Looking back on Renata from the Renata FSR

we will be in Edgewood by dusk' I thought, a lot less confident than the night before. I glanced back one last time as Renata disappeared behind us.

We arrived at the first of many intersections that were not in my mighty map book. Again panic set in. To make matters worse, my gas gauge, which I had not checked for some time, suddenly seemed to be racing its way toward the empty mark. Fortunately, on a last minute whim, I had thrown my half-full lawn mower gas can into the truck as we were leaving home two nights earlier. Its contents might power my lawn mower for hours, but my Toyota, despite its efficient mileage ratings, would not run far on the few remaining litres in that can.

Sighing heavily, I continued to ponder over my map book. I suddenly felt abandoned by it. It did not seem so mighty any more. I was accustomed to navigating in a world where maps were current, street signs were everywhere, and if I was really desperate I could always ask a passer-by for directions. These were suddenly non-existent luxuries in our current travel realm. Looking for clues on backroads can be like putting together a huge puzzle, aware that some pieces may or may not be missing and pieces of some other puzzle may or may not be intermixed with yours. It was then that the secret, surely known to many a seasoned backroad explorer when lost, revealed itself to me. I guessed. Or should I say, I made my first of many decisions that night based on hunches, and clues, if I thought they were such.

Steadily the trail climbed higher and higher. At a nondescript curve it developed into a modern logging road with wide shoulders and plenty of washboard surface, indicating heavy logging truck traffic. What a relief! Maybe I would make it as a backroad explorer yet. Even without my mighty map book, my educated guesses were taking us closer to civilisation.

We started passing large clear-cuts to our right. The cuts were so large and so far down the mountain side that Karen, sitting in the passenger seat, was actually experiencing vertigo from the endless plunge down to the lakeshore several kilometres below us now. The views into the Valhallas were magnificent; golden coloured snow patches in the alpine areas, as if set on fire by the setting sun, contrasted against the dark evergreen forests. It was a moment a landscape photographer waits all day for. I passed on the photo opportunity as I was too busy being concerned about our whereabouts and fuel dilemma.

After an hour or so of bouncing along, we came upon several

loggers on the side of the road. They were sprawled on lawn chairs, enjoying a plate of hot food. Behind them their fifth-wheel trailer was completely surrounded by pieces of huge logging equipment. Surprised, they looked up from their dinners.

'Thank you, Lord', I thought.

'Yes indeed,' they reassured me, 'this is the correct, and only, road to Edgewood. Just make sure you turn left at the Y-fork at the water tower.'

We graciously thanked them, and, wishing a good night, drove off slowly so as to not cover our divine help with a blanket of dust. We pressed on with renewed enthusiasm; there was little doubt, we were on our way to becoming savvy backroaders.

It was now dusk. We arrived at an intersection that we took as a T-intersection and not a Y-intersection as the loggers had described; we continued straight ahead. The trail now started to make its way back down to the lake, slowly at first with long sweeping curves, then more and more determined, with ever-tighter switchbacks. Obviously, we were on our way into Edgewood, in fact we could see some lights many kilometres ahead near the lake. Not soon enough as my gas gauge was far too close to the 'E' mark for my comfort.

'But what of the water tower' I thought out loud. We agreed that we had probably just missed it in the semi-darkness. Still something did not feel right to me. I pressed on, countless more switchbacks to navigate and generous amounts of brake pedal time. Just as we had earlier driven many kilometres up into the mountains, we now navigated many kilometres back down to the lake and into the comforts of a welcoming hamlet. With the last available daylight we rounded the last corner and had the lake in front of us. Just the lake...nothing else. No buildings, no people, no town, no Edgewood! We had come to a dead end at an abandoned logging yard.

Had we not been required back to work the next morning I would have camped right then and there. However, Karen did point out that we were out of food and water.

'That's actually not so bad,' I replied while turning around again. 'What really worries me is that we have no fuel left'.

I could tell that Karen suddenly was very unimpressed with my planning. The cab now felt deadly silent as I steered the truck back up the windy road. The dust from our descent still hung in the air and engulfed our lost little four-wheel drive and its weary occupants. As if following the ball at a championship tennis match, my eyes bobbed up and down between the windshield and fuel gauge. The needle was still going down! My neck and back were achy and tight. I moved my head from side to side, often squirming in my seat, arching my back in attempt to relieve my unease. My hands were sweaty, my jaw tense. For some reason the trail back up, now covered in total darkness appeared different. My tired mind suddenly questioned whether I had somehow taken a wrong branch after turning around by the lake. I forced that thought out of my brain. But the stress was mounting. I kept my gear shifting to a minimum to conserve our precious little fuel, the steep ascent not helping.

After the long climb, we arrived back at the T-intersection. I left the truck and walked around to make sure that this was the same intersection we had passed two hours previously; again there were no signs to offer clues or directions. Without further delay we headed down the other fork option, and hopefully towards Edgewood. Tensions now ran high with semi-heated exchanges between Karen and me. It certainly was not a matter of life and death. But feeling lost, on the verge of running out of fuel, having no water and not knowing where we were or where we were heading was taking its toll on our mood. Isolated camping beside a gravel road high in the Monashee Mountains was not an activity we were prepared for in this stage of our backroad exploration career. The chances of another vehicle that might happen by and lend us a hand were slim. My fuel gauge showed less than an eighth of a tank. I had never allowed it to be lower, and I did not know when I would actually run out of fuel. Suddenly, a set of headlight beams bounced along the deserted road in the distance ahead of us, like a ray of hope from far away.

'Get him to pull over,' Karen cried with relief. I stopped dead and repeatedly signalled the oncoming vehicle. It was a small pickup with two young men. The driver, his window already rolled down, looked up at me in anticipation.

'Do you know how to get to Renata?' he inquired, with a hesitant look, as if afraid to hear my answer. 'We have been driving down dead-end roads for hours since leaving Edgewood and are totally confused which way to proceed.

'Our map book doesn't seem correct,' he continued. He seemed exhausted, relieved to finally share his evening's plight with a fellow traveller. 'We are tree surveyors and need to start work near Renata tomorrow.'

'No problem', I laughed 'as long as you tell us directions to Edgewood.'

It was the young man's turn to laugh. We swapped instructions and with time running short wished each other good luck. We drove off in opposite directions, both eager to arrive at our night's destination. An hour later we finally bounced our way down the mountainside's rough logging trails into Edgewood. It was now midnight and the general store and only gas pump in town had long closed for the evening. Vernon, an hour or two away through the Monashee Pass on Highway 6, was the closest gas station open at this time of day. Highway 6 had infrequent traffic and running out of fuel there would be only an inconvenience compared to where we had just been. Wasting little time we agreed to push on.

I lost track of time. On a dark corner our trusty Toyota hit the wall as she started to buck and shake. The fuel gauge needle was so far to the left of 'E' it seemed to be coming up the other side; our fuel tank was completely empty. We coasted to a stop. With a flashlight I dug between the supplies in the back of the truck and retrieved the small gas can. Keera moaned loudly as I disturbed her sleep. Karen held the light while I emptied the can. Its precious contents echoed loudly as it all too quickly tumbled into the empty fuel tank.

At about 2 am, with the fuel gauge reading well to the left

of the 'E' mark again, we rolled into an all-night gas station in the Vernon outskirts. We had made it... just! As I filled up the truck it was two litres short of having a completely empty fuel tank again.

In Reflection...

Since this trip I have learned to always carry spare fuel during multiple-day backroad outings. I bring a small water filter to allow me to safely fill our canteen at any water source. Also, I learned that a black line on a backroad map book is often just that... a black line in the dirt or gravel that may or may not follow the route indicated in your map book. There are always additional roads which are not indicated on maps that keep you guessing. Road signs in the backcountry appear infrequently, if at all. Successful backroad navigating requires experience, gut feel and often a measure of good luck.

Speaking of good luck, I wonder if the two tree surveyors ever did make it to Renata.

Note:

On subsequent trips to Renata we have had the opportunity to visit the longest natural stone arch in Canada. This bridge, hidden in the mountainsides on the south side of Lower Arrow Lake several kilometres south-east of Renata, is 150 feet long and 100 feet above the ground. The hiking trail that leads to these natural phenomena is accessible only by boat. A summertime bed-and-breakfast is now available in Renata. Hosts George and Gloria graciously provide cottage accommodation for the weary backroad traveler, or just for the Nature-minded individual wanting to spend some quiet down time in comfort. Watch for the sign 'Creekside' next to the Renata bulletin board. For more information on either, including a water taxi to Renata, please contact Scottie's Marina on Broadwater Road outside Castlegar (250 365 3267).

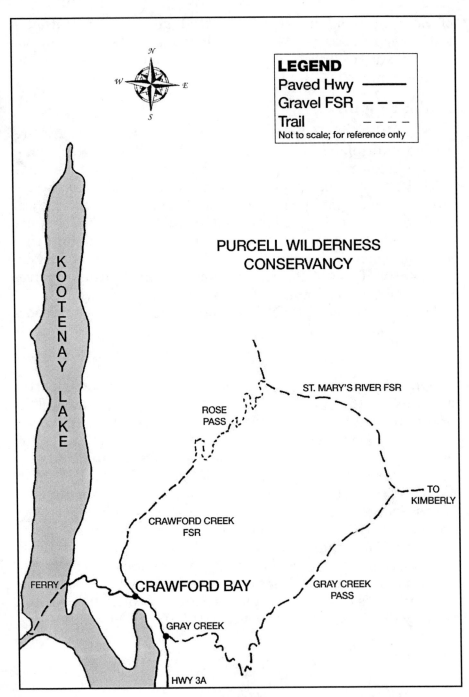

ROSE PASS

To Rose Pass or Not to Pass

...the front passenger tire landed heavily on top of the root, the entire vehicle then bounced out of control to the left. I was in trouble.

Difficult Trail Alert:

To cross Rose Pass by vehicle, expeditionary style four-wheel drive preparations and precautions may be necessary. Be prepared for trail reconstruction. If your vehicle is not equipped with a lift and locker, body panel damage and winching are likely. For personal safety do not attempt this pass without a support vehicle.

In the Beginning...

'I die willingly, because it is God's will. I have made my peace with Him. I am not guilty of the crime for which I stand here. My innocence may be, I pray God, proved some day. For all that, I forgive those who are the cause of my being here. If I have offended anyone, I beg forgiveness. I bid good-bye to all. I would like to say more but make it short because it is hard for me to stand here longer. I thank all who have been kind to me in my last days.'

With these words the condemned man, perfectly composed, walks firmly to the hangman's scaffold; for a moment he looks calmly down on the spectators assembled to see him die, then kneels and receives the last sacrament from the priest. As he stands up the priest asks him if he has anything more to say. The prisoner's lips move one last time and the priest, turning to the spectators, says, 'He says good-bye to all.' The priest then embraces and kisses the man on the cheek. As the executioner is adjusting the black cap and noose on the prisoner, the spectators raise their hats. The priest commences the last prayer in which he utters but a few sentences when the executioner suddenly exclaims, 'All ready,' and immediately pulls the lever which releases the bolts holding the trap door shut.

All is over.

It is shortly after 8:00 am, Nov 21, 1902. The spectators have gathered at the City Gallows in Nelson, a small bustling mining town in the heart of the Kootenays. The man publicly hung was Henry Rose.

Parts of the preceding passages were taken from archives that covered the 1902 trial and execution of Henry Rose, after whom Rose Pass is named.

Mountain trail passes have always captured my explorer's heart. This type of travel, from one watershed to the next across a mountain range without the need for backtracking, rarely exists outside the province's paved road systems. Rose Pass lies in the heart of the beautiful Purcell Mountains, bridging the West Kootenays and the East Kootenays. The remoteness of this century old pass, sense of history and caliber of challenge put this route in a league of its own. Surrounded by intimidating mountain names, such as Hungry Peak and Armour Peak, this largely forgotten pass came into recorded use in the 1860s. It allowed early European explorers into the Kootenay Lake Valley from the East. Natives had surely been using this pass long before then.

In the 1880s, a prospector, 'White Man Jim' Crawford, as the Natives called him, scaled the east-to-west Kootenay boundary and came to the area that now bears his name. Other prospectors followed. Henry Rose was one of them. Rose was born in Ottawa in 1838, of English and Scottish descent, and came to the Kootenays in 1890. He spent the early days of his prospecting career repeatedly crossing into the St. Mary's district from Crawford Bay over the Pass, and in so doing gave his name to it. The attending reporter at Henry's trial described him thus: 'Rose is by no means a beauty, but there were a

166

number of other men in the courtroom whom he could distance in a contest for points in personal appearance. He is a swarthy heavy-jowled man, but he has not a bad eye.'

As Henry moved through various employs and communities of the Kootenays, he earned the reputation as a man to be avoided when drinking. Perhaps his best-known and most entrepreneurial endeavour was his floating red light business on Kootenay Lake. This enterprise consisted of two log cabins, each assembled on a barge docked in Pilot Bay. Conveniently situated half way between the Pilot Bay Smelter and the local sawmill, this location allowed easy access for an endless stream of single men but was far enough away from town to avoid seriously raising any eyebrows. If business declined or complaints mounted, Henry could quickly relocate his floating bordello to other town sites along the lake.

Several years later Henry moved to Nakusp and bought a ranch. In June of 1902, during a drunken altercation, one of his business partners was beaten to death and the other was not expected to survive after having his skull fractured and losing an eye. Henry, the only suspect, spent several months in the Nelson jail awaiting his trial date. His court time was brief, only lasting five days. On the last day of his hearing the attending reporter commented, 'After a long and patient trial with every available space in the court room filled by all classes of the community, Henry Rose has been handed a sentence of the extreme penalty of the law… public hanging.'

Henry Rose was hung the next morning. Ironically, Henry's notoriety was doubly ensured when, shortly after his execution, public hangings were banned. Thus, Henry Rose became the last man to be hung in the City of Nelson.

Rose Pass was woven early into the strands of BC history. In 1894, the Government of BC considered the Pass important enough to spend money on it. The trail was improved on the Crawford Creek side to the summit. There is no record of further roadwork ordered since then.

The Pass has many interesting tales. In the summer of 1927, a group of twenty Boy Scouts from Kimberley spent five days hiking the then-prime grizzly bear habitat. During our first summer of attempting to locate the Pass, I learned that Scouts Canada had hiked the Pass again, to commemorate the original hike more than 70 years previous.

There is another tale from the 1930s about a large herd of sheep that were not allowed on the budding provincial road system by the authorities. The determined sheep owners, a family from the drought-stricken prairies, drove the entire herd over the tight confinements.

More recently in 2003, the Pass was part of the increasingly popular eco-adventure trekking sport, which saw contestants attempt to conquer Rose Pass on bikes, the most demanding portion of a 150-kilometre circuit.

Rose Pass is hidden, but not forgotten.

On the Trail... the First Attempts

My initial attempt to locate Rose Pass began through correspondence with Jud Barnes, the only person I knew who had travelled the Pass a decade earlier. Having explored other trails with Jud, I knew that he was gifted with an amazing memory. If anyone could remember the directions it was Jud.

On a sunny June day, with Jud's email directions in hand, Karen, Keera and I arrived by ferry in Crawford Bay. We had a few days left in our summer vacation. Confident that once in the general area I would have no problem locating the trail, I had foolishly left my map book at home.

Trying to gain further directions in the hamlet proved disappointing. The majority of locals thought I was referring to the Gray Creek Pass, a route several mountain peaks further south from Rose Pass. It is a well-built and maintained gravel logging road. Though steep, it grants passage through the Purcell Mountains as well. It is my suggestion to the reader to take this route if you plan to explore a backroad across the Purcells, unless you are comfortable with the conditions outlined in the 'Difficult Trail Alert' for Rose Pass.

Tom Lymbery, owner of the Gray Creek General Store, was most helpful. The store, owned by the Lymbery family since

1913, is situated on Chainsaw Avenue at the foot of Gray Creek Pass. I consider it a mandatory visit for any backroad explorer. The store stocks an incredible selection of items required for the outdoors and rural living.

Tom was not able to give us specific directions; rather, he indicated that a customer had mentioned to him that he had driven across the Pass 'sometime this year ', and that 'it was tough going at the top because of a rock slide'.

We spent our first night at a local campground, fully anticipating camping on the other side of Rose Pass by the following evening.

The next day we headed up the Crawford Creek FSR. The Kootenay mountain air in the forest shade was cool and refreshing despite the high noon temperatures. At a sharp curve in the road we headed uphill.

The trail came to an old creek crossing, constructed of several large logs tied together with rusted heavy steel cable. The bridge-like structure was embedded into the creek and not much use during peak runoff, but at this time of year it served its purpose well, as it had done for decades. Before proceeding across we stopped and took in all the different shades of plant life. On both sides of us the densely timbered mountains veered skyward. We stuck our heads out the truck cab and, straining our necks and backs, caught a glimpse of the top of the slopes. Ahead of us lay a narrow, curving valley, almost gorge-like. I savoured the evergreen scents carried by the dampness off the rushing creek, wishing I could take the aroma home with me.

A large silhouette caught my eye. At first I took it to be an old building but the contours were wrong. It was a mammoth tree trunk, camouflaged by the lush undergrowth. It had been felled high above ground level. Karen and I got out of our vehicle. While she stayed behind, I cautiously picked my way through eight-foot-tall devil's club, until I was touching the long dead monarch of the ancient Kootenay jungle. This fellow may have watched silently over this creek for hundreds of years, possibly more. I felt thrilled and saddened to see a tree of this size that had withstood the test of the mountains, the weather, all the elements combined and, above all, time, only to have its fibres ripped away one stroke after another by a steel saw. The notches on either side of the tree were still visible where the loggers of yesteryear had stuck their springboards into the bark of the tree, long before the mechanized world had entered the

Loggers of yesteryear armed with whipsaws and springboards

woods en-masse. Standing on their respective spring board, armed with a two-handled whipsaw or cross cut saw, the two men had surely sweated and toiled for days, before the enormous gnarled super structure of this giant surrendered to them and came crashing down to earth. A whole team of men and horses were required to move their prize to the mill.

Atop the long dead monarch

With difficulty, I climbed to the top of the stump. I felt like a curious child balanced on his grandfather's knee, somewhat unsure and content at the same time. Although it had been logged nearly a century earlier, through the sheer size of the remaining trunk I felt as though I could sense its presence and

171

the stature with which it was bestowed during its reign. It was by far the largest tree, dead or alive, that I had the pleasure of meeting in the Kootenays up until that time.

After we crossed the primitive bridge, the trail degraded. As it continued to erode, so did my confidence that this was Rose Pass. The route was so grown-in that large portions of the ground in front of our truck were obscured from our vision. I kept the truck centered in the small void where the competing brush from the left and right sides of the trail had not yet fully met. Tight switchback followed tight switchback in quick succession. This was indicative of early mining roads, another reason to discount this as the Pass. I later learned there had been a working mine in this area years earlier. This was likely the access road to that mine. We continued to inch and scratch our way up the narrow track carved into the steep slope, hoping to break out of the choking brush.

Finally, the alder thickets subsided, giving us a commanding view of the creek bed far below. I started to sweat: I realized we had not encountered a suitable turnaround for several kilometres. I could imagine more enjoyable activities than having to back down this trail, but with no other options we pushed onward.

The slide across the trail appeared in front of us as quickly as it had surely occurred. We stopped and got out. Nothing too serious, I thought. A log, two feet in diameter and two calf-size rocks blocked the way. The downed tree could easily be chainsawed, the rocks winched aside with the help of a snatch block. However, judging by the vegetation growth on the slide area, this event had occurred years previously. If Tom's customer had navigated through the Pass in the current year, the driver could not have come down this trail. Weighing all the evidence as to whether this was Rose Pass or not, we decided against going on. Of course reaching that decision was the easy part... now we had to turn our truck around on this tiny shelf road.

I walked back down the trail. I searched for the widest space possible, preferably one with a large tree on the downhill slope as an insurance policy should the trail shoulder crumble while we manoeuvred our four-wheel drive back and forth. The best possible spot was chosen and I returned to the truck. Karen was openly nervous, as was I, though I tried to appear calm.

Just then, a lone raven screeched ominously, circling just above us. In Native folklore the raven is seen as the messenger. As I climbed into the cab, I could not help but wonder about the timing of its arrival and its message.

Karen stood behind the vehicle and guided me back to the marked spot. I cut the steering wheel for the first of countless turns. I quickly realized that the trail simply was not wide enough. I climbed out, and, using our shovel and collapsible pick, we hollowed out a portion of the uphill embankment. Half an hour later, with aching palms and drenched in sweat, we had claimed an additional foot of real estate on the tiny road.

Back and forth, steering wheel cranked hard right, then hard left, over and over, gradually we nosed the truck around. The toughest part of this type of exercise is when the vehicle is turned ninety degrees to the trail direction or, in other words, the half way point; this is when the least amount of space is available in which to manoeuvre. At that stage you feel like, 'that's it, I am completely stuck now: can't go forward *or* backward', and you look for someone else to drive! I was only moving back and forth by a few inches once we reached that point. My rear tire carrier repeatedly contacted the insurance tree, but the trail shoulder, despite my driving right off it, held up well.

Ever so slowly we pointed the front of our little truck downhill. One last back up, one last full crank on the steering wheel and we had finally reversed our direction. Over an hour had elapsed. Triumphant and with a feeling of luxurious ease, we headed back down the track.

We reached the gigantic tree stump again by mid-afternoon and I studied Jud's directions once more, trying to make sense of where we were, annoyed with myself for not bringing my map book.

We returned to Crawford Creek, and followed an old trail that paralleled the creek eastward, up into the watershed. It

173

was relatively flat and straight. As our earlier trail had progressively deteriorated, so did this one. Jud had described a long valley to the left, for which I was on the lookout. Unfortunately, the trail side vegetation kept our visibility to near zero. Perhaps this was, in fact, the valley he had meant and the trail had drastically grown in since his visit.

Within a few kilometres of the trailhead we were halted by another washout. It had completely taken out the trail years earlier. We followed the only alternative, a sharp turn up to the right. This trail proved easy travelling with little bush growth and only occasional cross-ditches. As we gained altitude, we saw that we were indeed in a large valley into which side creeks emptied their precious resources. The trail switchbacked in a relaxed manner; the curves were easily navigated with a single turn. This was an old logging road built to allow large trucks and long loads to safely descend from the forest factories up above. This was a possible Rose Pass candidate.

We noticed bear scratches on a fir trunk, and then came across fresh bear scat on the trail. Perhaps the drone of our approaching engine had scared it into the thickets. Just then a flash of tan and black broke out of the underbrush and charged up the centre of the trail. For a brief second I was confused. How had our German Shepherd arrived in front of us? She always remained behind our truck while we were in motion; then I remembered that she was actually inside our truck. My brain finally focused. I recognised a bear cub, galloping ahead of us, as if leading us into battle. Then it stopped, turned around, looked at us with its dog-like head, and sat down, panting. The cub curiously watched us and let out a series of short squeals, as if asking us what our business was here. I had stopped as well; the engine idled. I fumbled for my camera. As I cranked my window open, I heard a huffing sound, hoarse and forceful. I paused from capturing my perfect Kodak moment. Our eyes scoured the brush ahead of us. We saw her simultaneously.

The mother with her shiny, black fur coat sat perched on the side of the trail thirty feet ahead. She let out another huff as she arched her head slightly skyward, similar to a wolf howl-

Mama Bear

ing. The sow's bruin suddenly took flight again, disappearing into the underbrush as quickly as it had appeared. I shut the engine off. Keera was sitting behind us in the cab; she let out a thin whimper. Her ears were straight as poles, her eyes focused intently on the mother bear. Instinct took over and our Shepherd remained quiet, though keenly observant, able to discern between perceived and actual danger. For the next fifteen minutes the black bear regularly let out her warnings. She often stood man-like on her hind legs, her gaze alert, her nose lifted up. She incessantly sniffed for danger, while her head rhythmically swept from side to side. She could not smell us inside the vehicle and she was obviously unsure how to proceed. All the same, she did not want her cub anywhere near us. Eventually, she calmed down, sat still for a while, and then, completely unhurried, sauntered into the trees. Now unseen to us, we heard her call a few more times. Her cub replied with a healthy 'bawl' and all was quiet in the neighbourhood of the woods again.

Enthused about our bear sightings we sat and talked for a long time. It was turning into early evening. We had hoped to be long over Rose Pass by now, having dinner in a secluded camp spot along St. Mary's River. Instead, with few daylight hours remaining, we were on a trail with no guarantees of its destination. We debated camping on the trailside for an early start in the morning. With a known bear family in the immediate vicinity we decided against it. Instead, we agreed to return to last night's campground in Crawford Bay. Perhaps the campground owner knew a local with knowledge of the Pass.

That night I slept restlessly, dreaming of Rose Pass. I saw myself as the raven which had visited us before our turn-around. Unfortunately, my dream did not reveal any promising leads on the exact location of Rose Pass.

The next morning I talked with the campground owner; she knew of the Pass but could not help us beyond that. Our original plan had been to depart for a leisurely drive home that day, but, surrendering to the explorer's spirit within us, we found ourselves driving deep into the Purcells once more.

Several hours later we arrived at the turn where we had sighted the black bears the day previous. We continued up the trail. The whole mountainside had been logged extensively, twenty or thirty years previous, and the grounds left bare. Human reforestation did not appear a priority back then.

For the majority of the time we had unlimited views into the Crawford Creek Valley as our four-wheel drive carried us ever onward and upward. This was looking more and more like Rose Pass.

As we approached the sub-alpine, our trail widened into a beautiful grassy meadow several acres in size with an amazing view of the valley and surrounding mountains. A long break here was mandatory.

I unloaded the camping chairs while Karen artistically prepared one of her trademark gourmet lunches on the tailgate.

We sat until long after lunch, captivated by the majestic quietude. Even if this trail did not lead to Rose Pass, this prominent spot alone was worth the trip up this trail.

Lacing up our hiking boots, we carried on by foot, and followed the trail at the eastern side of the meadow where it entered the natural green canopy. The last round of lumberjacks in this area had not felled the large fir and hemlock trees living here. They provided us with welcomed shade, and the trail, covered in soft green moss, made for a fairytale setting. We hiked for almost an hour when we were halted by a washout. Several hundred feet of mountain trail had slid into oblivion. Even hiking across the washout would be difficult, as the mountainside had been bared to bedrock in places. As in the other slides, this one looked several years old and, therefore, according to Tom's description, could not be Rose Pass. With a measure of sadness we retraced our footsteps. Even if this were not Rose Pass, it would have been a beautiful trail to follow to above tree line. With detailed maps I later determined that this may have been the access route to Cogle Pass, south of Rose Pass.

Back at the meadow we discussed staying for the night. Karen reminded me that we only had a couple of vacation days remaining. In addition, our current lack of Rose Pass options persuaded us to return to Crawford Bay, again. As we returned for the third consecutive night, the campground owner smiled sympathetically and commented on our tenacity.

I slept poorly that night, my mind pre-occupied with our quest. Admittedly, this was not the search for the Holy Grail, but my mind would not release. Why could I not find Rose Pass? Had Tom's customer given him misinformation about his year of travel through the Pass? Had one of the three washed-out trails actually been Rose Pass? All night long my brain ruminated with questions.

The next morning, far from rested, I knew I had to explore one more trail, even though it made absolutely no sense with respect to Jud's directions. I had to exhaust every conceivable option – I just had to know.

Karen finally agreed to forgo a relaxed two-day drive home to allow us to explore the Purcells one more time. The campground owner wished us luck, one more time.

Several hours later we crossed the Crawford Creek Bridge. I steered us up the logging road we had driven on our first day. But instead of turning off right I stayed on the main logging road. It had recently been upgraded with fresh fill, making for a bumpy but wide road surface, easily accommodating modern logging trucks. Corner after corner I expected to hit an active logging cut and heavy logging equipment. Corner after corner there was only more timber. This road continued on in this manner for several kilometres; the heavy woods around us prevented any views of the surrounding valleys or mountains.

Eventually, we reached the end of the road. It simply dead-ended. I followed a little foot trail for several hundred yards. Then it simply dead-ended as well. I could only assume this road had been improved for future logging activity. There were no other turnoffs. Our last Rose Pass option had expired, and so had our holiday time. Defeated, I turned the truck for our journey home.

Throughout the following winter I practised using my newly purchased GPS. Using the longitude and latitude information from this little technological marvel, in combination with local Forestry maps, I became proficient at route finding.

Armed with this new ally, I eagerly anticipated the next season of exploring, and, more specifically, finding Rose Pass.

...More Attempts

We planned a trip to the Crawford Bay area in July. Much to my enjoyment I discovered that Jud and three other four-wheelers were planning a trip to the Kootenays at the same time. We looked forward to meeting the other vehicles in Nelson, and attempting Rose Pass together.

It was another beautiful summer day as we crossed Kootenay Lake on the ferry. From the boat deck I stared at the magnificent Purcell Mountains; they seemed to beckon me like old friends. There was no other place I wanted to be at that instant. I wondered where the night would find us: on Rose Pass, over Rose Pass, in front of Rose Pass, or some place completely different.

After disembarking, we rounded the tight highway corners into Crawford Bay. A small black bear scampered across the pavement as we passed the gas station in the village. Nature was certainly on our doorstep in this part of BC.

We proceeded along Crawford Creek FSR until we came to the bridge and stopped for lunch. The July sun was becoming hotter by the minute, and everybody sought relief beneath the rustling cottonwoods along the creek. After lunch I showed Jud in the map book where, in our quest for the trailhead, I believed Karen and I had searched last year. He thoughtfully looked up into space, closed his eyes as if in meditation. After a long while he suddenly opened his eyes again and exclaimed, 'I think I know where you went wrong - follow me'.

As if having waited for Jud's command, the entire group was suddenly prepared to depart. The trucks shook off their dust. With Jud in the lead, and Karen and I behind him, we drove deeper into the Purcells. As on other trips with Jud, I had difficulty matching his speed on the backroads. Fortunately, he radioed back every time he took a turn to the right or left.

And then he was stopped at a tiny cut in the bushes. As we jumped out of our truck he proclaimed, 'This is it, this is the trailhead to Rose Pass!' It did not look any different than any other trailhead, yet, having finally located this elusive trail sent my explorer's heart into overdrive. The conquest of Rose Pass was still out of reach, as planted firmly in the middle of the trail in front of us was a sign which read, 'Road Washed Out, Closed to all Vehicular Traffic'!

By now the rest of the group had joined us. To say I felt crushed was an understatement. Desperately, I looked for a solution. I glanced at my feet, and found one.

'Okay, Karen and I will hike it,' I declared out loud. Karen looked over at me with raised eyebrows. The thermometer hovered mercilessly at 30°C, and here I was volunteering her for a hike up a 2000 metre high mountain pass.

'We'll just go for a bit,' I added sheepishly, pointing out that Keera was already out of sight on the trail. Karen laughed and said, 'OK, let's hike it for just a little bit.' The other group members were less enthusiastic about hiking at this time of day. They decided to turn their trucks around and explore other trails we had passed. We agreed to radio them when we had returned to our truck in order to meet up for the night's camp spot.

It did not take us long to question our decision to hike up a Kootenay mountain pass in the middle of that cloudless summer day instead of turning around with the others. The trail, though not aggressively steep, was steep enough. We struggled across a large washout, surely the reason for the closure sign. We came to a small waterfall and treated our scalps to a natural ice cold shower. Onward and upward we trekked. The surrounding mountain peaks gained in prominence as the valley floor grew distant. The trail side vegetation alternated between trees and shrubs. To keep from overheating, we allowed for frequent breaks. Keera would flop herself in a shady tree well, panting loudly, while Karen and I shared the canteen which we had refilled with fresh water at the falls. Our pace noticeably dropped as the elevation and temperatures climbed. After several kilometres Karen sighed, and, in Keera fashion, also flopped herself down in a shady tree well. 'That's it for me,' she stated emphatically. I knew I was not getting her any further.

I looked up the trail, helplessly; my view extended perhaps fifty feet before it was obscured by trees again. How much further was it? I did not know. I could see cliff sections higher up. I remembered Tom describing a rock fall at the top of the trail. Maybe that was it. It seemed so close and yet so far.

After a long rest together we headed back down to our vehicle. At the waterfall, we stripped and soaked our overheated bodies in the shallow pool – ahhh - Nature's revitalising energy at its finest!

Refreshed, we headed back to our truck. I contacted Jud on the VHF radio. He relayed the directions to their night's camp spot, a mountain ridge opposite of our current position.

That night our group relaxed around the campfire. It was one of those rare mountain evenings when, long after dark, it

Near the Rose Pass trailhead

was still warm enough for shorts and T-shirts. A gentle breeze blew in from the west, feeling as if it came straight from Hawaii. All around us was pure darkness, not a light to be seen from our lofty perch. The crystal clear Kootenay air magnified the galaxy clusters as they hung above our heads, seemingly close enough to touch. Karen and I announced that we would attempt another hike up Rose Pass with an early morning start to avoid the day-time heat. Our camping companions did not share our passion for reaching the summit of the Pass, or much preferred the air-conditioned comfort of their trucks, as they chose to drive on to other destinations in the Kootenays.

The next morning we said our good-byes and parted ways. Karen and I parked just off the trailhead as we had yesterday. However, we were better equipped with a lunch, power snacks and layered clothing. A stroke of genius had hit me overnight; I had my GPS powered up. As we knew the elevation of Rose Pass summit, we could judge our progress by our current altitude.

View onto Crawford Mountain from Rose Pass

When we reached the waterfall we knew we had made excellent time, and were grateful for the low morning temperatures. Soon we were hiking in unfamiliar surroundings. The higher section of the trail had never been logged and the virgin wood provided constant shade for our hike.

During a canteen break, I recalled the stories of the adventurous sheep and determined herders from long ago; they had descended this exact path. Their animal calls still seemed to echo throughout the tall timbers. I wondered if they lost any sheep off the trailside, or had the entire trail, prior to being logged, been guarded by evergreens.

As we gained altitude the trail became steeper. We reached the rock section. Little doubt this part would be extremely challenging to cross in a vehicle. Years of runoff waters had turned this section of the Pass into a washed out creek bed; jagged tire-size boulders and shale littered the trail as far as the eye could see. The steep embankments on either side gave the trail the feel of a shallow ravine. The rock bed continued past countless turns, each becoming steeper and tighter. The grade of the trail even made walking demanding. One step at a time we pressed on. Then, one last turn, one last stretch of boulders and there we stood. We had arrived at the top of Rose Pass, breathless and panting, our shirts wet with sweat. Yes, even Keera seemed elated that the climbing was finally over. With a heavy groan, she threw herself into the shade of an ancient hemlock. I gave her canteen water, which, between pants, she readily lapped out of my palm. Then, her thirst quenched, she relaxed to a tummy rub. Far below us lay Kootenay Lake, sparkling in the sun with snow capped peaks stretching far above the surrounding greens.

What a sight!

All our efforts forgotten, we gulped helpings of fresh air, relishing the visual fruits of our labour. Karen and I sat down on a big boulder and shared our canteen, our legs hung in front of us; my thoughts lazily drifted far back into the past. Surely, Henry Rose, during his treks over this rugged pass a hundred years earlier, had paused and rested in this exact spot. Happily dumping his pack onto the ground after an exhaustive ascent, he had likely enjoyed the sights with the same relish as we currently were, both for its scenic appeal and as a way-marker of progress. Perhaps he would quench his thirst from his own canteen. Maybe he sat on this exact boulder and smoked a pipe. I wondered if he reflected on that solitude the night before his execution. My knowledge of Henry Rose was limited to the coverage of his 1902 trial. However, I now knew he was obviously a man of determination and excellent physical fitness, to repeatedly climb through this steep mountain pass in his late fifties.

Grey Creek Pass - the sign says it all.

After a well-deserved rest, we began our long descent. That night we camped alone beside Crawford Creek, near the entrance to Rose Pass. We made numerous toasts to our success in reaching the summit and decided to drive over Gray Creek Pass the next morning in an attempt to locate the eastern trailhead of the Pass.

The next day, with surprisingly minimal soreness, we were on the road early. Opposite the Gray Creek Store we turned left off Highway 3A and geared down for our long windy trek up the Gray Creek Pass. The sights were almost as impressive as from Rose Pass, but constant logging traffic often clouded our views with dust.

At the St. Mary's River FSR intersection we turned left and followed the small road along the St. Mary's River. Several abandoned bridges were visible across the river but did not correspond to the GPS co-ordinates I had estimated.

At one point a section of the road had been washed away. Looking up the mountainside it was evident that a large snow avalanche the past winter had erased all vegetation in its path, including this part of the road. In fact, the avalanche was so powerful that it had barrelled up the opposite mountainside, causing equal havoc there. I used my shovel to move the smaller rocks to the side, and then carefully steered the truck through the debris field; entire trees that had been uprooted from above lay half buried in places and several car size boulders lay randomly scattered.

Eventually, we neared the desired GPS co-ordinates... and sure enough there it was, a turn to our left and a short drive to a bridge embankment. As Jud had described, the old logging bridge was missing; the ripped out sections had been unceremoniously dumped beside the trail on either side of the St. Mary's River and replaced by a ford. There were no closure signs in place. Surely visitors at this end of the Pass were far and few between.

With the aid of a large walking stick, I struggled across the fast flowing river, over three feet deep in places. On our own, and a long walk from help, we decided against driving across the ford to explore further. We turned our little truck for home, content to have likely found the eastern trailhead. Yet, we wondered if we would ever emerge from exploring Rose Pass on the other side of the river.

The St. Mary's River Ford

...The Final Attempt

The following summer I heard from a friend in Crawford Bay that Rose Pass had been 'repaired' for an Eco Adventure Race event. I was thrilled. Not sure to what degree the trail had been repaired, we planned a camping trip in late August with our friends Kari and Lucy. By this time the race would be over and the St. Mary's River would be near its lowest possible flow.

The weeks dragged by at an excruciatingly slow pace. At long last, we found ourselves back on the Kootenay Lake ferry. That night we camped near the western trailhead... and to my utter delight, the 'Road Closed' sign from last year had been removed. That night I felt like a child on Christmas Eve: the morning just could not come fast enough.

Day broke, and with no small impatience I charged through the morning's activities, helping wherever possible to hasten our trail departure.

Finally, our loaded trucks turned up the entrance to Rose Pass. We were on our way! The washout, which Karen and I had passed twice on foot last year, had been repaired with earth-moving equipment. Our trucks easily rolled over the fresh surface. It felt glorious to be finally driving up the Pass. We stopped at the refreshing waterfall to fill our canteens; no bath was needed this time.

As it was still early in the day we stopped at the severely brushed in areas, and with machetes and pruning shears spent several hours clearing the dense alder choking the trail. I was in the lead as we drove on and entered the virgin wood stands; numerous deadfall had been chainsawed recently, obviously courtesy of the race organizers, allowing us smooth sailing. Even the difficult sections that I remembered during our hikes the previous year were easily navigated. Our truck never required a stop, it never slipped, and it never even required a backup to pick a different line. We just headed skyward up the trail. After all the time spent, searching and waiting, the actual travel experience almost appeared anti-climactic. That was soon to change; we were nearing the summit.

We entered the ravine-like rock section. It looked as challenging as the year before. Our truck tires started to spin, our momentum faltered and soon our four-wheel drive had driven as far as it would go under its own power. The trail slope was too steep, the rocks too big and the altitude too high for the truck's carburetored engine. Behind us, I could hear the hiss and squeak of Kari's flexing suspension, frequently drowned out by grinding noises as his rubber tires and steel rims contacted rock. He was inching his own truck closer. The extreme slope of our truck made removing our seatbelts impossible. Our vehicle listed to the passenger side, our driver side tire unable to climb a large boulder. I talked to Kari over the CB. He agreed to park further behind us on the more level ground, get out and prepare our winch.

Carefully, he picked his way to the front of our truck bumper and un-spooled the winch cable. He wrapped the tree protector strap around a suitable fir and after hooking the winch cable to the strap loops, took my winch control and removed the cable slack. Then, one trigger pulse at a time on the winch control,

Winching near the Rose Pass summit

Kari inched us up onto the crest of the boulder. While he shouted directions, I steered and maintained the engine RPM, to keep the battery charged and the electric winch running at full capacity. Slowly, our faithful winch pulled our truck over that boulder and countless more, never missing a beat.

I was 100 percent dependent on the winch for forward movement. At times, the truck would slip sideways while attempting to be winched across a boulder. Kari would then have to release the winch cable tension, I would let the truck roll backwards several feet, and then try a new line up the boulder surface. If several new lines proved unsuccessful, we relocated the cable anchor point to obtain a new winching angle. We did not bother spooling in the excess cable as it was always immediately required. Kari looped it lasso style over his shoulder, looking like a dusty Kootenay cowboy who had just roped himself a stranded four-wheel drive.

Our progress was tedious, difficult and effective. Karen was able to release herself from under her seatbelt and was walking along side with Kari, helping move obstacles. Lucy helped spot. Eventually, the trail flattened out sufficiently to allow me to drive without the aid of the winch. Kari wrapped the winch cable, for potential later use, around my bulbar.

I saw one final boulder ahead of me. Recognizing this as the last turn before the top, I enthusiastically applied the throttle to power myself part-way up the right embankment and around the obstacle. Sitting on the driver side of the truck, I could not see the large tree root hidden under the grass to my right. It did not budge as my front passenger tire made the unexpected contact. The truck paused briefly, as if I had pulled in on the reins, the front right tire lifted itself into the air, and, after it landed heavily on top of the root, the entire vehicle then bounced out of control to the left. I was in trouble. I had hit the root with too much speed. The truck was going over on its side. I fought the ridiculous instinct to put my hand out the open window to brace the truck's fall. I gripped the steering wheel, felt myself tense up and closed my eyes. My world became quiet. For the shortest of time and the longest of time, the truck balanced precariously in the air, perched on the two driver side tires. Then the truck miraculously fell to the right again and remained upright. In fact, it landed on the far side of the root. I opened my eyes… whew, that was close! Alarmed, Karen and Kari made their way over to my window. I mumbled something about a stiff drink, barely made eye contact with them and, still in shock, drove on.

With loud cheers and huge smiles, we emerged at the top of the Pass; the close call of a minute ago further primed our adrenaline. It had taken several hours to winch our truck to the top. Kari and Lucy crawled back down the rock section to their waiting 4Runner. Their vehicle's off-road modifications allowed them to conquer the trail without the use of a winch; even so their better-equipped rig occasionally struggled to find the right line up the steep incline. Soon, Kari and Lucy too were parked on the clearing at the top of the Pass. We congratulated each other and savoured the endless views over lunch. Sitting on my large boulder, my thoughts drifted back to our hike last year and again to Henry Rose.

After an hour of rest we climbed into our trucks, reluctant to leave the lands of the West Kootenays behind, yet eager to follow the century-old pass into the East Kootenays.

When the majestic St. Mary's Alpine region came into view a photo stop was required, its distant location making it no less impressive.

The trail now took on a different flavour. It followed an old skidder path, becoming twisty, with large mud holes and washouts. We came to the edge of a gigantic clear cut, providing us views to the valley bottom far below us. The trail branched right and left. Instinct told me to go right. Tight, off-camber turns had to be navigated as we wound our way across the logging battlefield, the trail deeply rutted by the large machinery now long gone. Several of the turns were so steep they made me nervous, my recent near-rollover flashing through my mind. Because I was in the lead, I often stopped to ensure that we were still on the main trail, not a side branch that would dead end. I often guessed. After countless switchbacks we entered the tree canopy again, all without a single backtrack. I quietly congratulated myself.

Several kilometres further we passed a precarious trail washout that granted us mere inches between our outside tires and the crumbling trail edge; without maintenance, this washout would soon make this trail impassable.

Further on, we rolled up to a 'tank trap' type washout: a deep 'V', five or six feet deep, and not much wider at the top. I jumped out of the truck. Had we driven this far only to be turned

The majestic St. Mary's Alpine

back so close to the end? The ditch looked impossible to drive through with a long wheel base vehicle like our truck. 'What do you think?' I asked Kari, who had caught up behind me.

'No problem,' he replied with his standard answer. I should have known better! After another minute of contemplation I climbed back in the cab. I looked at Karen and she shot me a smile of encouragement. We braced ourselves, expecting, hideous grinding sounds, as the truck's entire undercarriage would surely hang up on the ditch edges. Then, before we knew it, our front tires were pulling us onto the far side, all without a single bump... or maybe I had not noticed in my excitement. Kari followed close behind us, and also encountered no problems. It was our lucky day.

Two old trails led in different directions, I picked the less overgrown route. Curve after curve my impatience mounted...had I taken the correct branch at the washout? Had I taken the correct branch at the top of the Pass? Would this

191

trail exit at the St. Mary's River ford by the old bridge embankment or dead end? Would we have to turn around and
drive back out the entire pass? As the curves continued so did
my questions. The tall trailside brush prevented any views
outside the natural corridor. I felt trapped.

Entering the St. Mary's Valley

And then the St. Mary's River appeared, ever so briefly,
between the brush. One last turn and we emerged precisely at
the old bridge embankment and ford. I let out a resounding
'YES'. Jubilant we leapt out of the truck and broke into a cel-
ebration jig. Kari and Lucy pulled up and laughed at our
behaviour; aware of the amount of time and energy we had
invested in the last three years attempting to cross Rose Pass.

Once our excitement wound down, we agreed to make camp
for the night and tackle the river crossing in the morning. Tired
out from the day's adventures, we hit our sleeping bags just
after sunset. I slept deeply, my nightly restlessness on previous Rose Pass trips finally absent.

I awoke at daybreak. Our camp was quiet as no one else was up. I carefully unzipped the tent fly. Keera's big wet nose immediately greeted me as I crept out. In the distance I could hear a woodpecker hammering on his future home. Two squirrels chased one another across our campsite. I stretched and looked east. The sky behind the towering mountain was a pale pinkish-blue, speckled with small wispy clouds; it would be another beautiful hot August day in the Kootenays.

Our German Shepherd followed me down to the riverbank. Startled, two feathered inhabitants noisily sought refuge in the air as we approached their hideout. Their loud cries of discontent seemed out of place in the peaceful air. The ducks circled us, and then disappeared down the river to find a new sanctuary. Like a blanket, the mountain stillness covered us again. I stepped into the chilling river. Keera followed me, had a long drink, and then, satisfied, lay down on the bank, content to watch me from there. As I washed, two large dragon flies greeted me, chasing one another with unbridled enthusiasm, up and down, back and forth, never tiring. They reminded me of Karen and myself in our hunt for Rose Pass.

I joined Keera back on the gravel bank, stretched out and watched as the sun emerged from behind the mountaintops. I closed my eyes. The valley temperature immediately climbed; it felt beautifully warming on my skin after the cold bath. I broke into a big grin immenselly grateful that we had safely crossed this beautiful and historic pass, after all the time and effort spent in locating it. It had taken a number of attempts, but, as with most worthwhile endeavours, it proved deeply rewarding. I felt utterly, absolutely and completely relaxed. A fabulous sense of well being surged over me. I enjoyed it for the longest time.

After breakfast and clean up of our campsite, we guided our two trucks down to the ford. We waded through the waters to verify its depth and become familiar with any tough spots. Fortunately, both our trucks were winch-equipped, so we could help extricate one another if necessary.

In the lead, our truck met little resistance, other than sliding sideways on several large rocks in the deeper section, as we steered the final leg of our Rose Pass adventure. Despite the late time of year the river water fully submerged our tires; crossing this river any earlier in the summer, especially during a high runoff year, would be difficult. Kari waited for me to fully cross before following. He took a different line and met with difficulty climbing up the far bank. Around the old bridge debris we drove and emerged onto the St. Mary's logging road. It had taken several years and numerous trips, but Rose Pass had finally consented to 'being passed'.

In Reflection...

Countless images from our search for Rose Pass and our eventual crossing are indelibly stamped in my mind's eye. Like a series of treasured picture books they are available to me upon request: the gigantic old growth tree stump, the alarmed raven circling us during our perilous turn-around, the protective mother bear huffing warnings to her cub, the shining galaxies hanging in the black Kootenay night, the small refreshing waterfall half-way up the Pass. And, of course, a vision of Henry Rose, over a century ago, his pack at his feet, sitting on that boulder, taking in the view of the Purcells, breathing heavily after his hike, surely feeling alive and free at the top of 'his' Pass. These and more are mine. And when I am stuck in everyday life, deep in suburbia, when my surroundings chatter incessantly, it is these images that I draw upon, gather energy from and I feel grounded again.

Bibliography

Arrow Lakes Historical Society, Circles of Silver. (Friesens, Altona, MB 2001)

Barlee, N. L., Gold Creeks and Ghost Towns. (Hancock House, Surrey, BC 1984)

Barlee, N. L., Canada West Magazine. (N. L. Barlee, Surrey, BC 1982)

Barman, Jean, The West beyond the West. (University of Toronto Press, Toronto, ON 1991)

Bostwick, Mark, Four Wheeling in the BC Interior. (Harbour Publishing, Madeira Park, BC 1997)

Bostwick, Mark, The Four Wheeler's Companion. (Harbour Publishing, Madeira Park, BC 1988)

Bowering, George, Bowering's BC. (Penguin Books, Toronto, ON 1996)

Burrows, Roger, Railway Mileposts: BC Volume II. (Railway Milepost Books, Vancouver, BC 1984)

Clemson, Donovan, Outback Adventures (Hancock House, Vancouver, BC 1974)

Kelowna Daily Courier, Kelowna Public Library Archives. Kelowna, BC

Lindsay, F.W., The Caribou Dream. (The Vernon News, Vernon, BC 1972)

Nelson Daily News, Nelson Public Library Archives. Nelson, BC

Ramsey, Bruce, Barkerville. (Mitchell Press, Vancouver, BC 1961)

Ramsey, Bruce, Ghost Towns of British Columbia. (Mitchell Press, Vancouver, BC 1963)

Sanford, Barrie, McCulloch's Wonder – The Story of the Kettle Valley Railway. (Whitecap Books, West Vancouver, BC 1978)

Shewchuk, Murphy, Coquihalla Country. (Sonotek Publishing, Merritt, BC 1990)

Shewchuk, Murphy, Fur, Gold and Opals. (Hancock House, Surrey BC 1975)

Turnbull, Elsie, Ghost Towns and Drown Towns of West Kootenay. (Heritage House, Surrey, BC 1988)

Glossary

Adit: Mine shaft entrance.

All Terrain Tires: Many tire manufactures produce *All Terrain* tires. These types of tires are more aggressive than a street truck tire but less aggressive than a mud tire.

Air Down: Four wheelers often 'air down' their tires at the beginning of a rough trail to soften the ride of their vehicle. An aired down tire is less prone to trail damage as it folds or conforms more readily to the objects it rolls over. This practice can significantly increase traction under certain trail conditions and increase tire life. Many tire manufacturers now design tires with side lugs, specifically to improve traction when aired down.

CB: Citizens Band two-way radio (27MHz HF Band). Used for vehicle to vehicle communication over short distances. No licence is required to operate a CB radio. Many four-wheelers in BC use and monitor CB channel 4.

Cross Ditches: Ditches dug perpendicular to the logging road edge. Their purpose is to channel and prevent runoff waters eroding sections of the roadbed. Roads are cross-ditched or deactivated when logging access will not be required for the foreseeable future. Some trails may be cross-ditched to discourage travel.

Flume: An inclined man-made channel for carrying water.

FSR: Forest Service Road. Roads built by the Ministry of Forests or logging companies to access forested areas.

FSR Main: The major Forest Service Road from which all other spur roads branch. The Main is usually wider and often maintained. Spurs are narrow and see little or no maintenance.

Deactivation: See cross-ditch.

GPS: Global positioning system. An electronic device that receives signals from satellites orbiting the earth. It allows for accurate navigation by supplying information on speed, distance travelled, location, etc. almost anywhere in the world.

HAM: Term for an individual who is licensed for Amateur Radio Bands. HAM's are now often called Amateur Radio Operators.

Lift: Means of adding undercarriage clearance to a vehicle. Added lift will usually allow larger tires to be installed for additional clearance. Most lifts are expensive modifications but can dramatically improve off-road performance at the expense of on-road handling.

Locker: A means of added traction control by having both the driver and passenger tires on the same axle receive power simultaneously or be 'locked' together. Many four-wheel drive vehicles actually only have one or the other tire of a given axle under power, even when 4WD is activated. Lockers can be air, cable or electronically activated, or be in constant lock.

Main: Abbreviation for FSR Main.

Mud Terrain Tires: *Mud Terrain* tires are designed with large lugs to enable the tire to self-clean mud and smaller rocks from its tread. They are usually noisier and less responsive on pavement, especially when wet, and are more expensive than regular truck tires.

Pull Strap: Also known as a recovery strap. A specially designed strap which converts the kinetic energy of the towing vehicle momentum into spring potential energy. This energy is converted towards pulling out the stuck vehicle. Purchase only quality pull straps from a knowledgeable Off Road Supplier to ensure that you receive the proper weight rating for your application.

RAC: Radio Amateurs of Canada. Many four-wheelers obtain their Amateur Radio licence to allow use of higher power two-way radios and thus improved communication over CB radios.

Roller Fairlead: The part of a winch that allows the winch cable to evenly exit or enter the winch drum. It also allows the cable to move at extreme angles to the winch drum.

Shackle: Also known as 'D' Rings. The safest means of connecting straps and the winch cable together. Purchase only quality shackles from a knowledgeable Off Road Supplier to ensure that you receive the proper weight rating for your application.

Slag: Rock taken from a mine and discarded, usually within close proximity of the mine. See tailings.

Snatch Block: A device used to change the angle of a winch cable pull and/or increase the pulling power of a winch.

Tree Protector Strap: A tree protector is looped around the anchor tree when winching. It protects the tree from the winch cable pressure damage. It is a large strap, usually three or four inches wide and at least six feet in length, with one loop at either end. A shackle is attached through the loops and the winch cable hook can then be attached to the shackle.

Tailings: The residue left over after mining: the rocks and boulders not found to contain any desirable metals.

VHF Radio: Very High Frequency (30MHz to 300MHz). Many four-wheelers with an RAC licence will use VHF radios for long distance truck to truck communications, repeater communications and to monitor logging and Forestry channels, usually 150 MHz to 155MHz.

Winch: A motor that turns a gear arrangement, which turns a drum that reels in cable. Most winch-equipped four-wheelers in BC have electric winches, though hydraulic winches are available as well. A winch can be permanently mounted, usually on the front of the vehicle, or removable for front and rear mounting capabilities and theft prevention. Winches are marvellous tools that can be life threatening if misused.

Water Bars: See deactivations.

Parting Picture

Thanks for listening.

ISBN 141205903-8